BOOKS BY OGDEN NASH

I'm a Stranger Here Myself
Good Intentions
Many Long Years Ago
Versus
Family Reunion
The Private Dining Room and Other New Verses
You Can't Get There from Here
Verses from 1929 On (selections from published works)
Everyone but Thee and Me

FOR YOUNG READERS

Parents Keep Out: Elderly Poems for Youngerly Readers
The Christmas That Almost Wasn't
Custard the Dragon
Custard the Dragon and the Wicked Knight
The New Nutcracker Suite and Other Innocent Verses

You Can't Get There From Here

OGDEN NASH

You Can't Get There From Here

DRAWINGS BY
MAURICE SENDAK

Boston · LITTLE, BROWN AND COMPANY · *Toronto*

LIBRARY OF CONGRESS CATALOG CARD NO. 57-7838

FIFTH PRINTING

Published simultaneously in Canada
by Little, Brown & Company (Canada) Limited

PRINTED IN THE UNITED STATES OF AMERICA

To Edith Haggard,
good friend, peerless agent, and brutal taskmaster,
with affectionate gratitude

Most of these poems first appeared in the following magazines and are reprinted through the courtesy of *What's New* (Abbott Laboratories), *Coronet, Good Housekeeping, Harper's Bazaar, Harper's Magazine, House & Garden, Look, McCall's Magazine,* the *Magazine of Fantasy and Science Fiction,* the *New Yorker, New York Herald Tribune TV and Radio Magazine,* the *Saturday Evening Post,* the *Saturday Review, True, the Man's Magazine.*

CONTENTS

You Can't Get There From Here

ANYBODY FOR MONEY?
or
JUST BRING YOUR OWN BASKET

Consider the banker.
He was once a financial anchor.
To pinch our pennies he would constantly implore us,
And if we wouldn't pinch them ourselves, he would pinch them for us.
Down to thrift he was always admonishing us to buckle,
Reminding us that many a mickle makes a muckle.
When with clients he was closeted,
He was attempting to convince them that everything ought to be made do, worn out, eaten up, or deposited.
In a word, if you wanted to catch up with the Joneses or bust,
You couldn't do either with the connivance of the First National Pablum Exchange & Trust.
Yes, bankers used to be like Scrooge before he encountered the ghost of Marley,
But along came TV and now they are Good-Time Charlie.
The jingle of coins multiplying at 2 per cent per annum has given way to the jingle of the singing commercial,

And their advertisements, implying that anyone who doesn't turn in his this year's car for a next year's model with all the latest excessories and borrow the difference from them is a frugal old fogy, range from the supplicatory to the coercial.
The way some people sing whiskily,
Bankers are singing fiscally.
Everything is hey-nonny-nonny,
Come in and get some money.
That bankers have only themselves to blame for the recent wave of holdups and embezzlements I think highly probable,
They are behaving so provocatively robbable.

BIRTHDAY ON THE BEACH

At another year
I would not boggle,
Except that when I jog
I joggle.

SO I RESIGNED FROM THE CHU CHIN CHOWDER AND MARCHING CLUB

The thing about which I know the least
Is the inscrutable East.
Neither is my ignorance immutable,
I find that every hour the East grows more inscrutable.

Day by day
I memorize pithy witticisms beginning "Confucius say."
I retire to leafy bowers
And immerse myself in *Kai-Lung's Golden Hours,*
In the evening I beat assiduously on a gong,
Picking out "Slow Boat to China" and "Why Did I Tell
You I Was Going to Shanghai?" and "Chong He
Come from Hong Kong."
In a valiant effort the inscrutable Oriental mind to ex-
plore
I have lost a fortune at mah-jongg to an inscrutable
Pekingese puppy who lives next door,
All to no avail;
Scrutably speaking, I am beyond the pale.
I have only one accomplishment about which I would
write home to Mother:
I can tell at least one Celestial from at least one other;
I can tell you, for a modest price,
The difference between a mandarin waving his hat over
a prostrate palanquin bearer and a mandarin sit-
ting on a cake of ice.
Do you want to know, really and truly?
Well, the first mandarin is fanning his coolie.

NATURE–WALKS

or

NOT TO MENTION A DOPPING OF SHELDRAKES

I. THE SQUID

What happy appellations these
Of birds and beasts in companies!
A shrewdness of apes, a sloth of bears,
A sculk of foxes, a huske of hares.
An exaltation 'tis of larks,
And possibly a grin of sharks,
But I declare a squirt of squid
I should not like to be amid.
Skin divers boldly swim through sepia,
But I can think of nothing creepier.

2. THE OSTRICH

The ostrich roams the great Sahara.
Its mouth is wide, its neck is narra.
It has such long and lofty legs,
I'm glad it sits to lay its eggs.

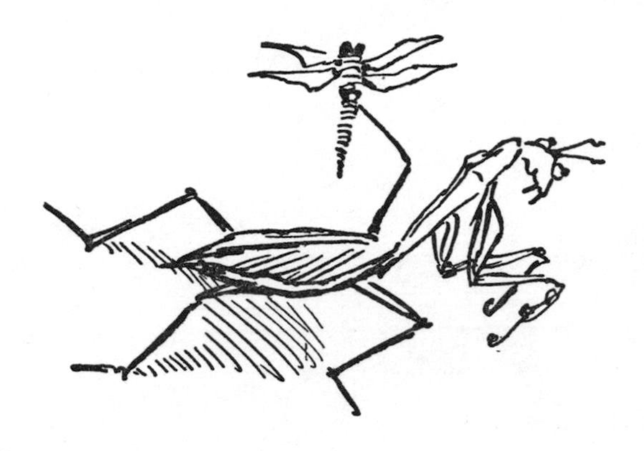

3. THE PRAYING MANTIS

From whence arrived the praying mantis?
From outer space, or lost Atlantis?
I glimpse the grim, green metal mug
That masks this pseudo-saintly bug,
Orthopterous, also carnivorous,
And faintly whisper, Lord deliver us.

4. THE ABOMINABLE SNOWMAN

I've never seen an abominable snowman,
I'm hoping not to see one,
I'm also hoping, if I do,
That it will be a wee one.

5. THE MANATEE

The manatee is harmless
And conspicuously charmless.
Luckily the manatee
Is quite devoid of vanity.

6. THE SQUAB

Toward a better world I contribute my modest smidgin;
I eat the squab, lest it become a pigeon.

RING OUT THE OLD, RING IN THE NEW, BUT DON'T GET CAUGHT IN BETWEEN

I. FIRST CHIME

If there is anything of which American industry has a
superfluity
It is green lights, know-how, initiative and ingenuity.
If there is one maxim to American industry unknown
It is, Let well enough alone.
Some people award American industry an encomium
Because it not only paints the lily, it turns it into a two-toned job with a forward look and backward fins and a calyx trimmed with chromium.
I don't propose to engage in a series of Lincoln-Douglas debates,
But take the matter of paper plates.
The future of many a marriage would have been in doubt
But for paper plates, which have imparted tolerability to picnics and the maid's day out,
But the last paper plates I handled had been improved into plastic and they are so artistic that I couldn't throw them away,
And I ended up by washing them against another day.

Look at the automotive industry, how it never relaxes;
It has improved the low-priced three so much that instead of a thousand dollars they now cost twenty-nine seventy-five, not including federal and local taxes.
Do you know what I think?
Ordinary mousetraps will soon be so improved that they will be too good for the mice, who will be elbowed out by mink.

2. SECOND CHIME

That low keening you hear is me bemoaning my fate;
I am out of joint, I was born either too early or too late.
As the boll said to the weevil,
Get yourself born before the beginning or after the end, but never in the middle of, a technological upheaval.
I am adrift, but know not whether I am drifting seaward or shoreward,
My neck is stiff from my head trying to turn simultaneously backward and forward.
One way I know I am adrift,
My left foot keeps reaching for the clutch when the car has an automatic shift.
Another way that I am adrift I know,
I'm in a car that I've forgotten has a clutch and I stall it when the light says STOP and again when the light says GO.
I find that when dressing I behave as one being stung by gallinippers
Because half my trousers are old style and half new and I am forever zipping buttons and buttoning zippers.
I can no longer enjoy butter on my bread;

Radio and TV have taught me to think of butter as "You
know what" or "The more expensive spread."
I am on the thin ice of the old order while it melts;
I guess that perhaps in this changing world money
changes less than anything else.
That is one reason money is to me so dear;
I know I can't take it with me, I just want the use of
some while I am here.

MS. FOUND UNDER A SERVIETTE IN A LOVELY HOME

. . . Our outlook is totally different from that of our American cousins, who have never had an aristocracy. Americans relate all effort, all work, and all of life itself to the dollar. Their talk is of nothing but dollars. The English seldom sit happily chatting for hours on end about pounds.

— NANCY MITFORD in *Noblesse Oblige*

Dear Cousin Nancy:

You probably never heard of me or Cousin Beauregard or Cousin Yancey,

But since you're claiming kin all the way across the ocean, we figure you must be at least partwise Southern,

So we consider you not only our kith and kin but also our kithin' couthern.

I want to tell you, when Cousin Emmy Lou showed us your piece it stopped the conversation flat,

Because I had twenty dollars I wanted to talk about, and Cousin Beauregard had ten dollars he wanted to talk about, and Cousin Yancey didn't have any dollars at all, and he wanted to talk about that.

But Cousin Emmy Lou looked over her spectacles, which the common people call glasses,

And she offered us a dollar to stop talking about dollars and start talking about the English upper classes.

Cousin Beauregard wanted to know why the English aristocracy was called English when most of their names were French to begin with,

And now anybody with an English name like Hobbs or Stobbs has to accumulate several million of those pounds they seldom chat about, to buy his way in with.

Cousin Yancey said he could understand that — the St. Aubyns beat the hell out of the Hobbses in 1066 — but there was a more important point that he could not determine,

Which is why the really aristocratic English aristocrats
have names that are translated from the German.
Cousin Emmy Lou is pretty aristocratic herself; in spite
of her weakness for hog jowl and potlikker, she is
noted for her highborn pale and wan flesh,
And where most people get gooseflesh she gets swan flesh,
And she said she thought you ought to know that she had
been over the royal roster
And she had spotted at least one impostor.
She noticed that the Wicked Queen said "Mirror, mirror
on the wall" instead of "Looking glass, looking
glass on the wall," which is perfectly true,
So the Wicked Queen exposed herself as not only wicked
but definitely non-U.
We finally agreed with you that the English aristocracy
has a tough row to hoe, but it has one spectacular
solace:
When there is unrest overseas and all other envoys have
failed, it can call on a charming royal personage,
whereas we can only offer John Foster Dulles.
After that, we all loosened our collars
And resumed our conversation about dollars.

DON'T BE CROSS, AMANDA

Don't be cross, Amanda,
Amanda, don't be cross,
For when you're cross, Amanda,
I feel an albatross
Around my neck, or dank gray moss,
And my eyes assume an impervious gloss.
Amanda,
Dear Amanda,
Don't be cross.

Do not frown, Amanda,
Amanda, do not frown,
For when you frown, Amanda,
I wamble like a clown,
My mouth is stuffed with eiderdown,
And I spatter coffee upon your gown.
Amanda,
Dear Amanda,
Do not frown.

Don't clam up, Amanda,
Amanda, do not clam,
For when you clam, Amanda,
I don't know where I am.
What is it that I did you damn?
Shall I make amends for a sheep, or a lamb?
Amanda,
Dear Amanda,
Do not clam.

Please be gay, Amanda,
Amanda, please be gay,
For when you're gay, Amanda,
The stars come out by day,
The police throw parking tags away,
And I want to kick up my heels and bray.
Amanda,
Dear Amanda,
Please be gay.

OAFISHNESS SELLS GOOD, LIKE AN ADVERTISEMENT SHOULD

I guess it is farewell to grammatical compunction,
I guess a preposition is the same as a conjunction,
I guess an adjective is the same as an adverb,
And "to parse" is a bad verb.
Blow, blow, thou winter wind,
Thou art not that unkind
Like man's ingratitude to his ancestors who left him the
English language for an inheritance;
This is a chromium world in which even the Copley
Plazas and the Blackstones and the Book Cadillacs
are simplified into Sheratons.
I guess our ancient speech has gone so flat that we have
to spike it;
Like the hart panteth for the water brooks I pant for a
revival of Shakespeare's *Like You Like It.*
I can see the tense draftees relax and purr
When the sergeant barks, "Like you were."
— And don't try to tell me that our well has been de-
filed by immigration;
Like goes Madison Avenue, like so goes the nation.

SIC SEMPER MR. SHERMAN'S TEMPER
or
KINDLY PLACE YOUR ORDER IN ENGLISH

I have a friend named Mr. Sherman who is far from
dodderin',
But he lives old-fashioned instead of moderun.
He believes that the terminology of drinking has long
been complete,

And it needs new wrinkles like Manhattan needs a hole
in the street.
He thinks the phrase whisky on ice
Is both descriptive and precise,
So of rocks he keeps a store
Which he gathered on the stern New England shore,
And when guests ask for bourbon on the rocks they get
bourbon on the rocks and they squint at their
bourbon on the rocks jitterily
Because he fulfills their request literally,
And when they clamor for that new favorite, bouillon
on the rocks, his eyes are so moist that he melts
them with them,
And then he dips the rocks in bouillon and pelts them
with them.
As for the folksy he-men who slap him on the back and
bellow for bourbon and branch water, they don't
do it a second time or a third,
He takes them at their word;
He has imported a dozen Mason jars of genuine branch
water from the Ozarks, and every serving con-
tains three tadpoles and a crawfish,
After receiving which even a governor of Tennessee
would switch to Scotch and soda and behave a little more standoffish.

AND HOW KEEN WAS THE VISION OF SIR LAUNFAL?

Man's earliest pastime, I suppose,
Was to play with his fingers and his toes.
Then later, wearying of himself,
He devised the monster and the elf,
Enlivening his existence drab
With Blunderbore and Puck and Mab.
A modern man, in modern Maryland,
I boast my private gate to fairyland,
My kaleidoscope, my cornucopia,

My own philosopher's stone, myopia.
Except when rationalized by lenses,
My world is not what other men's is;
Unless I have my glasses on,
The postman is a leprechaun,
I can wish on either of two new moons,
Billboards are graven with mystic runes,
Shirts hung to dry are ragtag gypsies,
Mud puddles loom like Mississipsies,
And billiard balls resemble plums,
And street lamps are chrysanthemums.
If my vision were twenty-twenty,
I should miss miracles a-plenty.

THE SOLITUDE OF MR. POWERS

Once there was a lonely man named Mr. Powers.
He was lonely because his wife fixed flowers.
Mr. Powers was a gallant husband, but whenever he wished to demonstrate his gal*lant*ry
His beloved was always out with six vases and a bunch of something or other in the pantry.
He got no conversation while they ate
Because she was always nipping dead blossoms off the centerpiece and piling them on her plate.
He could get no conversation after meals because if he happened to begin one
She would look at the mantel and wonder if she shouldn't switch the small fat vase with the tall thin one.
Yes, even when she wasn't actually fixing flowers there was no forgetting about them,

Because before fixing them she was busy cutting them,
and after fixing them she was busy fretting about
them.
Mr. Powers began to shave only once a week because no
one cared whether his chin was scratchy;
He felt as lonely as *Cavalleria* without *Pagliacci.*
Finally he said Hey!
I might as well be alone with myself as alone with a lot
of vases that have to have their water replenished
every day,
And he walked off into the dawn,
And his wife just kept on refilling vases and never no-
ticed that he was gone.
Beware of floral arrangements;
They lead to marital estrangements.

A BRIEF GUIDE TO RHYMING,

or

HOW BE THE LITTLE BUSY DOTH?

English is a language than which none is sublimer,
But it presents certain difficulties for the rhymer.
There are no rhymes for orange or silver
Unless liberties you pilfer.
I was once slapped by a young lady named Miss Goringe,
And the only reason I was looking at her that way, she
represented a rhyme for orange.
I suggest that some painter do a tormented mural
On the perversity of the English plural,
Because perhaps the rhymer's greatest distress
Is caused by the letter *s*.
Oh, what a tangled web the early grammarians spun!
The singular verb has an *s* and the singular noun has
none.
The rhymer notes this fact and ponders without success
on it,
And moves on to find that his plural verb has dropped the
s and his plural noun has grown an *s* on it.
Many a budding poet has abandoned his career
Unable to overcome this problem: that while the ear
hears, the ears hear.

Yet he might have had the most splendiferous of careers
If only the s's came out even and he could tell us what his
ears hears.
However, I am happy to say that out from the bottom of
this Pandora's box there flew a butterfly, not a
moth,
The darling four-letter word d-o-t-h, which is pronounced
duth, although here we pronounce it doth.
Pronounce? Let jubilant rhymers pronounce it loud and
clear,
Because when they can't sing that their ear hear they can
legitimately sing that their ear doth hear.

CAN I GET YOU A GLASS OF WATER?
or
PLEASE CLOSE THE GLOTTIS AFTER YOU

One trouble with a cough,
It never quite comes off.
Just when you think you're through coughing
There's another cough in the offing.
Like the steps of a moving stair
There is always another cough there.
When you think you are through with the spasm
And will plunge into sleep like a chasm,
All of a sudden, quickly,
Your throat gets tickly.
What is this thing called a cough

That never quite comes off?
Well, the dictionary says it's an expulsion of air from the lungs with violent effort and noise produced by abrupt opening of the glottis,
To which I can only reply, Glottis — schmottis!
Not that I reject the glottis theory, indeed I pride myself on the artistry
Of my glottistry,
But there is a simpler definition with which I freely present you:
A cough is something that you yourself can't help, but everybody else does on purpose just to torment you.

CHACUN À SON BERLITZ

French is easy.
At speaking French I am the champ of the Champs
Elysee,
And since I can speak Parisian without a flaw,
I will tell you why the crows, or les corbeaux, always win
their battle against the scarecrows: it's on account
of their esprit de caw.

I SPY
or
THE DEPRAVITY OF PRIVACY

My voice is a minor one, but I must raise it;
I come not only to bury privacy, but to praise it.
Yes, this is my long farewell to privacy;
Democracy seems to have turned into a sort of Lady
Godivacy.
We are living in an era by publicity bewitched,
Where the Peeping Toms are not blinded, but enriched.
Apparently it is not so much talent that creates the celebrity
As his or her highly publicized excursions into virility or muliebrity.
The very paper in which the fishmonger wraps up his mackerel and flounders
Reeks with the temporary attachments of glamorous alley cats who would have been once ostracized as tramps and bounders.
Keyhole-itis is contagious, and I fear that by our invasion of the privacy of the people who pay money for their privacy to be invaded,
Well, we are ourselves degraded;
And now that we can't leave the privacy of public personalities alone

We end up by invading our own.
What puts a neighbor's teeth on edge?
Your growing a hedge.
He is irked because he can't see what you're doing on your own lawn, raising tulips,
Or swigging juleps,
And curiosity is what he is in his knees up to,
And also exhibitionism, because he not only wants to know what *you* are doing, he wants you to know what *he's* up to,
So he has a picture window to look out through that he never lowers the blinds on, so you can't help looking in through it,
And you are forced to observe the nocturnal habits of him and his kin through it.
Things have reached a pretty pass; even my two goldfish, Jael and Sisera,
Complain that they have no more privacy than a candidate's viscera.
Well, privacy is a wall,
And something there is that does not love it: namely, the Pry family, Pauline and Paul.

THE NYMPH AND THE SHEPHERD
or
SHE WENT THAT–A–WAY

Few things are less endearing than a personal comparison,
But I know a lady who is very like the elusive mother of
Mr. Milne's James James Morrison Morrison.
She would be a perfect wife could she but be restrained
by a leash or a fetter,
Because she has the roving tendencies of an Irish setter.
Her husband assists her from the cab and stops to pay
the fare,
And when he turns around she isn't there,

She is a hundred yards off, blithe as a flock of linnets,
And in a fair way to do the mile under four minutes.
He assists her from the train and by the time he has caught a porter she is at the top of the moving stairway,
And again to do the mile under four minutes she is in a fair way.
She shoots ahead of him in London crowds and leaves him behind fumbling with lire in Pisa,
Despite the fact that he is in sole possession of all the travelers' checks and their joint passport and visa.
If in the Louvre she exclaims, "Oh, look at the Mona Lisa!" and he pauses to look at the Mona Lisa,
By the time he has looked she is three corners and forty masterpieces away, and himself alone with the same old money and passport and visa.
Sometimes he is touched and flattered by her faith in him, but mostly he feels like Queen Victoria's chair,
Which Queen Victoria never looked behind at before she sat down, because she just knew it would be there.

THE EMANCIPATION OF MR. POPLIN
or
SKOAL TO THE SKIMMERLESS

To tragedy I have no addiction;
What I always say is there's enough trouble in real life without reading about it in fiction.
However, I don't mind tears and smiles in a judicious blending,
And I enjoy a stormy beginning if it leads to a halcyon ending.
That is why I like the story of Byron Poplin, who prided himself on never having had an allergy, because he considered allergies a form of hypochondria,
And then he fell in love with a beautiful hat-check girl named Andrea.
He would check and recheck his hat to the tune of six or seven quarters an evening in his eagerness to survey her allures,
But all she ever said was, "This yours?"
He followed her here and there and all he got was there a No and here a No,
And he was as frustrated as Cyrano.
She grew more gelid as he grew more torrid,
And he developed a rash on his forehead.
There was melancholy music in his heart,

But his forehead looked like a raspberry tart.
He attributed the rash to unrequited love and so he felt like the hero halfway through an operetta by Romberg,
But a dermatologist told him it was merely the result of an allergy to the lining band of his Homburg.
Mr. Poplin is now anathema to cloakroom attendants because he goes around hatless as well as cloakless, but he is both allergy- and Andrea-free,
And by not buying his hat six or seven times a night he has been able to pay the dermatologist's modest fee;
Indeed, he eventually saved enough quarters to buy a convertible, in which he drives bareheaded and happy as an earl,
So let us leave him without further ado and also without a hey-nonny-nonny and a hat-check girl.

THE BUSES HEADED FOR SCRANTON

The buses headed for Scranton travel in pairs.
The lead bus is the bolder,
With the taut appearance of one who greatly dares;
The driver glances constantly over his shoulder.

The buses headed for Scranton are sturdy craft,
Heavy-chested and chunky;
They have ample vision sideways and fore and aft;
The passengers brave, the pilots artful and spunky.

Children creep hand in hand up gloomy stairs;
The buses headed for Scranton travel in pairs.

They tell of a bus that headed for Scranton alone;
It dwindled into the West.
It was later found near a gasoline pump — moss-grown,
Deserted, abandoned, like the *Mary Celeste.*

Valises snuggled trimly upon the racks,
Lunches in tidy packets,
Twelve *Daily Newses* in neat, pathetic stacks,
Thermoses, Chiclets, and books with paper jackets.

Some say the travelers saw the Wendigo,
Or were eaten by bears.
I know not the horrid answer, I only know
That the buses headed for Scranton travel in pairs.

FEE FI HO HUM,
NO WONDER BABY SUCKS HER THUMB

I don't know whether you know what's new in juvenile literature or not,
But I'll tell you what's new in juvenile literature, there's a new plot.
I grew up on the old plot, which I considered highly satisfactory,
And the hope of having stories containing it read to me restrained me occasionally from being mendacious or refractory.
There were always two older sons and a youngest son, or two older daughters and a youngest daughter,
And the older pair were always arrogant, selfish rascals, and the youngest was always a numskull of the first water,

And the older ones would never share their bread and cheese with little old men and women, and wouldn't help them home with their loads,
And ended up with their fingers caught in cleft logs, or their conversation issuing in the form of toads,
And the young numskulls never cared what happened to their siblings, because they had no family loyalty,
They just turned over all their bread and cheese to elderly eccentrics and ended up married to royalty, which I suppose explains what eventually happened to royalty.
That was admittedly not a plot to strain the childish understanding,
But it was veritably Proustian compared to the new plot that the third generation is demanding.
Whence these haggard looks?
I am trapped between one lovable grandchild and her two detestable favorite books.
The first is about a little boy who lost his cap and looked everywhere for it, behind the armchair and inside the refrigerator and under the bed,
And where do you think he found it? On his head!
The second is about a little girl who lost one shoe on the train, and until she found it she would give the porter and the other passengers no peace,
And finally where do you think she found it? In her valise!

A forthcoming book utilizing this new plot will tell the story of a child who lost her grandfather while he was reading to her, and you'll never guess where she discovered *him.*

Spang in the middle of Hans Christian Andersen and the Brothers Grimm.

AN ENTHUSIAST IS A DEVOTEE IS A ROOTER
or
MR. HEMINGWAY, MEET MR. STENGEL

Into the Grand Canyon of the Colorado
Drop, my boon companion, the word "aficionado."
Brand me as provincial, hoot me for a jingo,
Hint that I'm an Oedipus to love my mother lingo,
On my reputation cast a nasty shadow,
Adamant you'll find me anent "aficionado."

Never may I languish prey to xenophobia.
Sydney Smith admire I, and Luca della Robbia,
And should Fate transport me into regions foreign
I could wear a chlamys, I could wear a sporran;
Yet, gazing at the Parthenon, strolling through the Prado,
Art lover I might be, but no aficionado.

Monosyllabic Master, whither are we heading
Since you thrust upon us this verbal featherbedding?
You who freed the language of fetters euphuistic,
You who taught us terseness, muscular and fistic,
You whose prose is soldierly, Spartan and Mohican —
Why employ ten letters to do the job that three can?

This reproachful tribute to a first-class writing man
Comes from no aficionado,
Just
A loyal
Fan.

THE EDUCATION OF ATHELNY JONES
or
ARE THERE MORE RADIOS IN HACKS THAN HACKS IN RADIO?

Once there was a man named Athelny Jones and he drove a hack,

And although he yearned for culture he had no means of acquiring culture so he called his female passengers "Sister" and his male passengers "Mac."

Well, how could he achieve culture when, whether he was cruising or standing, hired or hireless,

The law forbade him a TV set in his hack — yes, even so much as a wireless?

He was cut off from all forms of culture such as the liberal arts and medicine and sports and science,

So he never got to know who was John's Other Hopkins or who had just knocked off the Giants.

He had reached a cultural nadir because, not having heard of Bennett Cerf, he had to make up his own jokes when he joked

(Three of which will appear in the new Cerf volume, *Stop Me If It's Constitutional*), and then one day the ban on radios in hacks was revoked.

At once a spate of culture overwhelmed Athelny's ears, if not his vision;

He was subjected to the broadening influence of crooners
crooning Parisian.
He was wafted into a glamorous *vie en rose* of amorous
ruses,
Of small cafés and chestnut trees and carrousels and ren-
dezvouses.
In a short time he was so Gallicized
That even when he exclaimed such exclamations as Hein!
and Zut alors! they weren't italicized.
He was quick to call a dick a flic.
Today the humblest visiting Hoosier
Steps out of Athelny's hack feeling like a sophisticated
Moulin Rouger.
In all this great city it is the only hack
In which the passengers are addressed as "Mam'selle Sis-
ter" and "M'sieu Mac."

GO AHEAD, IT WILL DO YOU GOOD
or
HER EYES ARE BIGGER THAN HIS STOMACH

Most of the literature of insurance to me is cryptic and mystic,
But when I read it I am given pause by a certain actuarial statistic.
Yes, just as some people are fascinated by fisticuffs,
I am fascinated by one group of actuarial statisticuffs,
Which proves that although husbands have the temporary satisfaction of being stronger,
Their wives live an average of four years longer.
I haven't read any reports from Oslo or the Skagerrak or the Kattegat,
But those are the figures from Hartford, Connecticut.
It was not always thus,
As anyone knows who has made a tour of Colonial graveyards on foot or by bus.
There lies Ebenezer who at the age of 91 entered into the Kingdom of Heaven,
Preceded at decent intervals by his wife Abigail, 23, his wife Prudence, 26, his wife Martha, 31, and his wife Priscilla, an old crone of 37.

Please stand by to award me a sprig of laurel or a glowing
calendulum;
I think I have discovered what reversed the pendulum.
Today's housewife has more horror of waste than under-
standing of the innards of her mate,
And she insists that he eat up everything on his plate.

Be he fifty-dollar-a-week clerk or fifty-thousand-dollar-a-
year banker,
He is cowed into cramming down that last three cents'
worth of orts for which he does not hanker.
A victim of the thrift and culinary pride of his loving but
misguided wife,
Although he is already full, he eats up everything off the
plate and four years off his life.
The gist of the statistic may be found right there:

The empty plate leads to the empty chair.
Madam, I assume it is your desire to extend your husband's life, not to diminish it;
What's left on the plate, buy some swine and let them finish it.
Swine are happy their graves with their teeth to dig,
And anyhow what's four years to a pig?

YOUR LEAD, PARTNER, I HOPE WE'VE READ THE SAME BOOK

When I was just a youngster,
Hardly bigger than a midge,
I used to join my family
In a game of auction bridge.
We were patient with reneging,
For the light was gas or oil,
And our arguments were settled
By a reference to Hoyle.
Auction bridge was clover;
Then the experts took it over.
You could no longer bid by the seat of your pants,
The experts substituted skill for chance.

The experts captured auction
With their lessons and their books,
And the casual week-end player
Got a lot of nasty looks.
The experts captured auction
And dissected it, and then
Somebody thought up contract,
And we played for fun again.
It was pleasant, lose or win,

But the experts muscled in,
And you couldn't deal cards in your own abode
Without having memorized the latest code.

We turned to simpler pastimes
With our neighbors and our kin;
Oklahoma or canasta,
Or a modest hand of gin.
We were quietly diverted
Before and after meals,
Till the experts scented suckers
And came yapping at our heels.
Behold a conquered province;
I'm a worm, and they are robins.
On the grandchildren's table what books are displayed?
Better Slapjack, and *How to Win at Old Maid.*

In a frantic final effort
To frivol expert-free,
I've invented Amaturo
For just my friends and me.
The deck has seven morkels
Of eleven guzzards each,
The game runs counterclockwise,
With an extra kleg for dreech,
But if you're caught with a gruice,
The score reverts to deuce.
I'll bet that before my cuff links are on the bureau
Some expert will have written *A Guide to Amaturo.*

THE RING IN GRANDFATHER'S NOSE

1. NOT MENDACIOUS, JUST GRACIOUS

Two pairs of grandparents
Babble o'er the cradle,
Serving up the syrup
With a silver ladle.
Says each pair to t'other pair,
"The tot takes after your side!"
If either pair believed itself,
There'd be a lot more suicide.

2. THE PUSHOVER

My grandchild, who, when walking, wobbles,
Calls dogs Bow-wows, and turkeys, Gobbles.
Today I called a cow Moo-moo;
She's got me talking that way too.

3. THE SABOTEUR

My pretty new watch
Goes tickety-ticket,
Whenever I wind it
It chirps like a cricket.
The second hand
Hippety hippety hops
Till shaken by baby;
Then pretty watch stops.

4. YOU'RE ONLY OLD ONCE

The midnight chime rings loud and clear;
Where are my friends of yesteryear?
Well, one I know is at the fights,
One watching chorus girls in tights,
One playing poker at the club,
And one orating in a pub,
One sleeping quietly as a kitten.
And where am I? I'm baby-sitten.

HO, VARLET! MY TWO CENTS' WORTH OF PENNY POSTCARD!

One thing about the past,
It is likely to last.
Some of it is horrid and some sublime,
And there is more of it all the time.
I happen to be one who dotes
On ruins and moats;
I like to think on the days when knights were bold and ladies demure,
And I regret that my strength is only as the strength of nine because my heart is not one hundred per cent pure.
However, I also like to think on periods other than the Arthurian,
I like to think on the period when most types of invertebrate marine life flourished and coral-reef building began — namely, the Silurian.
I believe that Cro-Magnon caves and huts on stilts in lakes would make nifty abodes,
And I am given to backward glances o'er traveled roads.
Because I am one in whom Waverley romanticism prevails,
I guess that is why I am fascinated by the United States mails.

The attitude of the Post Office Department is much to
my taste;
It holds that posthaste makes post waste.
In these drab days when trains and airplanes fill the
grade crossings and skies by the million,
The mails are still carried by dusty couriers on fat palfreys, riding pillion.
So as a dreamy-eyed old antiquarian I hereby, dear Post
Office Department, express my appreciation to you:
Thanks to whom we can diurnally eat archaic and have
it, too.

GOOD-BY NOW
or
PARDON MY GAUNTLET

Bring down the moon for genteel Janet;
She's too refined for this gross planet.
She wears garments and you wear clothes,
You buy stockings, she purchases hose.
She says That is correct, and you say Yes,
And she disrobes and you undress.
Confronted by a mouse or moose,
You turn green, she turns chartroose.
Her speech is new-minted, freshly quarried;
She has a fore-head, you have a forehead.

Nor snake nor slowworm draweth nigh her;
You go to bed, she doth retire.
To Janet, births are blessed events,
And odors that you smell she scents.
Replete she feels, when her food is yummy,
Not in the stomach but the tummy.
If urged some novel step to show,
You say Like this, she says Like so.
Her dear ones don't die, but pass away;
Beneath her formal is lonjeray.
Of refinement she's a fount, or fountess,
And that is why she's now a countess.
She was asking for the little girls' room
And a flunky thought she said the earl's room.

IT WOULD HAVE BEEN QUICKER TO WALK
or
DON'T TELL ME WE'RE THERE ALREADY

Let us call her Mrs. Mipping, but her name is legion,
And she is to be found in any taxi helping to congest any
congested region.
Human experience largely consists of surprises superseding surmises,
And most surprises are unpredictable, which is why they
come as surprises.
There is one surprise, however, that is as predictable as a
statement by a Republican or Democratic national
chairman or a picture window in a pre-fab,
And that is the surprise of Mrs. Mipping when she gets to
where she was going in a cab.
In fact, she gets two surprises at a clip:
The first, that she has reached her destination, and the
second, that she is expected to pay for the trip.
If she is heading down to 5th Avenue and 52nd Street she
doesn't start to assemble her packages at 57th or
55th or even 53rd,
But when the cab pulls up at her corner she flutters like
a bewildered bird,
And she proceeds to gather up her impedimenta

While the faces of the several dozen drivers blocked behind her turn magenta,
And only then does she realize that a figure has been registered on the meter,
And she is thunderstruck as by an explosion of gunpowder, which is largely composed of sulphur, charcoal and saltpeter.
Down go the packages on the seat again,
And she fumbles in her bag for her purse and fumbles in her purse for change and finally hands the driver a ten.
By the time the transaction is completed it is growing dark,
And traffic is backed up all the way to Central Park.
I believe that the Traffic Commissioner could soon iron out the situation as smooth as silk
Simply by opening charge accounts with the taxi companies for Mrs. Mipping and her addlepated ilk.

COME ON IN, THE SENILITY IS FINE

People live forever in Jacksonville and St. Petersburg and
Tampa,
But you don't have to live forever to become a grampa.
The entrance requirements for grampahood are comparatively mild,
You only have to live until your child has a child.
From that point on you start looking both ways over your
shoulder,
Because sometimes you feel thirty years younger and
sometimes thirty years older.

Now you begin to realize who it was that reached the height of imbecility,
It was whoever said that grandparents have all the fun and none of the responsibility.
This is the most enticing spiderweb of a tarradiddle ever spun,
Because everybody would love to have a baby around who was no responsibility and lots of fun,
But I can think of no one but a mooncalf or a gaby
Who would trust their own child to raise a baby.
So you have to personally superintend your grandchild from diapers to pants and from bottle to spoon
Because you know that your own child hasn't sense enough to come in out of a typhoon.
You don't have to live forever to become a grampa, but if you do want to live forever,
Don't try to be clever;
If you wish to reach the end of the trail with an uncut throat,
Don't go around saying Quote I don't mind being a grampa but I hate being married to a gramma Unquote.

EXIT, PURSUED BY A BEAR

Chipmunk chewing the Chippendale,
Mice on the Meissen shelf,
Pigeon stains on the Aubusson,
Spider lace on the delf.

Squirrel climbing the Sheraton,
Skunk on the Duncan Phyfe,
Silverfish in the Gobelins
And the calfbound volumes of *Life.*

Pocks on the pink Picasso,
Dust on the four Cézannes,
Kit on the keys of the Steinway,
Cat on the Louis Quinze.

Rings on the Adam mantel
From a thousand bygone thirsts,
Mold on the Henry Millers
And the Ronald Firbank firsts.

The lion and the lizard
No heavenly harmonies hear
From the high-fidelity speaker
Concealed behind the Vermeer.

Jamshid squats in a cavern
Screened by a waterfall,
Catered by Heinz and Campbell,
And awaits the fireball.

AND THAT'S WHY I ALWAYS TAKE THE OAKLAND FERRY TO BEVERLY HILLS

I think that if you get an arresting idea you should stick
to it,
But I also think you can overdo it.
With this in mind, there is someone we might take a moment to ogle:
Namely, the cinema mogul.
Through the decades in which he has reached financial
and artistic peaks
He has retained two *idées fixes.*
The first is that although for many years diesel and electric locomotives have been what the railroads and
I and you choose,
He prefers to picture the Twentieth Century and the
Broadway as being hauled by choo-choos.
The second is that when you approach New York from
no matter what part of the nation,
Why, you end up in Grand Central Station.
Whether you get on at Great Neck or Atlantic City or
Nyack or New Orleans, where do you get off?
Grand Central.
It's elementral.
This bland denial of the existence of the Pennsylvania
Amounts to monomania.

When Colonel James Mason of G–2 entrains in Washington for Saks Fifth Avenue with designs so new that they are almost germinal,
Where is he decanted? Grand Central Terminal.
Did the P.R.R. route a special train for him via Harrisburg, Buffalo, and Syracuse?
I cannot say. I find it most mysteracuse.

ALL'S BRILLIG IN TIN PAN ALLEY

I. I SAW EUTERPE KISSING SANTA CLAUS

Thomas Lovell Beddoes inquired, "If there were dreams
to sell, what would you buy?"
He never got a reply,
But to whom was he talking?
Probably to people who had never even seen a dream
walking.
As an Inquiring Reporter,
Thomas Lovell Beddoes should have posed his question
in another quarter.
Had he sought his answers just below where Broadway
bisects the lower Fifties,
He would have come up with some nifties.
In the Brill Building lobby
Dream buying is a profitable hobby.
It is there that the imaginative tune carpenter or smith
Can purchase a shadow to walk down the avenue with.

There lurks the phrase that neither grammar nor plausibility apply to;
There he may find tulips to tiptoe through and blackbirds to say bye-bye to;
There amid the lyrical crowds
He may lay in a supply of sunshine with which to paint the clouds.
(Or, if it is not immediately available at the Brill,
Anyone can direct him to the Old Master Painter on a faraway hill.)
There prowls the dream prospector in search of the ultimate strike:
A melody that a pretty girl is like.
It was there the other day that I dreamed I saw Stephen Foster;
He couldn't have looked loster.

2. GOOD NIGHT, SWEET MIND

May I remark, at the risk of being called an egghead or New Dealer,
That the characters in many of our popular songs are fair game for the nearest mental healer?
The evidence is voluminous,
And the fact that these people are invariably boys and girls rather than men and women is not the least ominous.
My mostest favorite couple is a brace of young lunatics who, hand in hand,
Are wandering at large in what they are pleased to designate a Winter Wonder*land*.

(In the Brill Building this kind of nomenclature
Is second nature.)
In the middle of a meadow these two mooncalves not only conceive the notion of building a snowman,
They proceed to call him Parson Brown, and when he asks them if they are married they answer, No, man.
Realizing that this abrupt answer may have wounded the sensibilities of Parson Brown,
Why, they hasten to assure him that he can unite them when he is in town.
By this time the bluebird — and don't ask me what bluebird — has been replaced by a new bird, and they romp off through the snowbanks,
Depositing their happiness, I imagine, in no banks.
Well, I'll go my way, let them go theirs,
But I can't help wondering if Parson Brown isn't the same holy man who has subsequently made a tidy wad officiating at the round-robin marriages of our ruby-throated playgirls and madcap millionaires.

THE LITERARY SCENE

I

The Marquis de Sade
Wasn't always mad.
What addled his brain
Was Mickey Spillane.

II

Some words, like ugly courtiers,
Should lag behind the portieres.
Here's two such hippopotami:
Ambivalence, dichotomy.
I deprecate their prevalence,
Dichotomy, ambivalence.
Why do the learned quarterlies
Such couthless cant immortalize?

III

In imperial boudoirs
The heroine noudoirs.
For so mimsy a babe
The womraths outgrabe.

IV

How many miles to Babylon?
Love-in-a-mist and Bovril.
Are there more Sitwells than one?
Oh yes, there are Sacheverell.

V

In a kindlier age, writers ate high on the hog
If they wrote books entitled *Lincoln's Doctor's Dog.*
Now I hear that a scientist in a Yorkville rathskeller
Has devised an infallible title for a modern best seller.
It's so obvious that when I repeat it I cry *"Ach Himmel!"* —
How to Think Positively While Climbing an Undersea Mountain to Interview a Female.

ANYBODY ELSE HATE NICKYNAMES?

These are the times when all our feminine notables are beautified
And, unfortunately, the times when all our masculine notables are cutified.
This is the day of public diminutives,
Of Virginny instead of Virginiatives.
You don't remember Addison Sims of Seattle, you remember Addie,
Who today drives a Caddie.
Kenneths are few but Kennys are many,
Even John Benjamin becomes Jack Benny.
Then, as we choo-choo further along the trackies,
All the Jacks become Jackies.
O tempora! O mores! Or rather, O tempy, O mory!
O Binnorie, O Binnorie!
O idols with mouths of babes and feet of straw!
O shades of Jackie L. Sullivan and Jackie J. McGraw!
I'm so confused I don't know where I are;
I shall curl up on the hearth with my two Kilkenneth cats, Bo and Zsa.

THE BARGAIN

As I was going to St. Ives
I met a man with seven lives;
Seven lives,
In seven sacks,
Like seven beeves
On seven racks.
These seven lives
He offered to sell,
But which was best
He couldn't tell.
He swore that with any
I'd be happy forever;

I bought all seven
And thought I was clever,
But his parting words
I can't forget:
Forever
Isn't over yet.

THE COMIC SPIRIT
or
NEVER SAY DIE, SAY KICK THE BUCKET

Let us consider the comic artist, whose jolly fancies our colorless existence adorn;
Let us consider in particular one who was incontrovertibly to the profession born.
He began with an advantage that neither thieves nor Fate could from him filch:
His name was Elmer Zilch.
He gave early indications of his latent comic self
By hooking cakes from window sills, and piling chairs on top of each other to reach the jam jar on the kitchen shelf.
He never attended circuses but by crawling slyly under the tents,
And he saw many a ding-dong ball game through the knotholes in the Yankee Stadium fence.
As a freckle-faced lad he grew comparatively rich
By catching salmon on a bent pin and selling them to pudgy salmonless millionaires outfitted by Abercrombie and Fitch.
Later he grew comparatively poor by giving the young brothers of girls he sat on sofas with a quarter to run along and play,

Little realizing that they had no interest in the doings of anybody crazy enough to sit on a sofa with their sister and were already on their way.

Small wonder then that his bride never got to wear the snappy travel ensemble for which she had paid more than a mess of pottage;

His artistic instinct drove him to snatch her from the reception and carry her, bridal gown, veil and bouquet, across the threshold of their honeymoon cottage.

Small wonder that he pretended to break a tooth on her first biscuit and called her family odd kin;

Small but happy wonder that she his quietus made with a rolling pin, which is more comical than, and just as lethal as, a bare bodkin.

THE MAN ON THE SHELF

Your lists of books for desert island reading,
Forgive me if I pass them by unheeding.
Forty years back, or add a couple to it,
I was on a desert island and never knew it,
A happy island rimmed by sea-blue time,
Easy and artless as a children's rhyme.
Who could retire to dreams of change or travel
When horseshoes crunching on the driveway gravel
Might any moment start the breathless guess,
Is it only the butcher — or is it Adams Express?
Dull bundles from McCreery's or — who can tell —

Green-wrapped and stamped with Schwarz's familiar
bell?
And who could list ten books for special praises
When books grew wild like buttercups and daisies?

Just So Stories and *Jungle Books,*
And groups of Goops in jingle books,
And Beatrix Potter all in a row,
And *Westward Ho!* and *Ivanhoe,*
Bab Ballads gay as hurdy-gurdy,
And *Men of Iron,* and *The Princess and Curdie,*
And *Helen's Babies'* comical capers,
And *Slovenly Peter* and *Peterkin Papers,*
And, omnivorous being the growing boy,
Five Little Peppers, and *Fauntleroy.*
If I was Pythias and Dracula Damon,
There was plenty of Henty and Stanley Weyman,
The Wind in the Willows, with Rat and Mole in it,
And the Peter Newell book with the hole in it,
Rolfe in the Woods, and Kirk Munro,
Tom Brown, and Eric, and *Stalky & Co.,*
The White Company, Little Black Sambo,
Fairy books red and blue and rainbow,
Legends of Gorgons and Polyphemus,
And *The Rose and the Ring,* and *Uncle Remus.*
I've been cast away with poor Ben Gunn
And the jolly *Swiss Family Robinson,*
And Tom and Huck with their tattered galluses.
The Three Musketeers and both the Alices,

Oliver Twist and *Tanglewood Tales,*
So list me no list of new-fanglewood tales.

I've lost my island and I've lost my books,
And people blame me for my backward looks.
They explain to me with condescending unction
That children's books must perform some useful func-
tion.
I hold that *Peter Rabbit* is paramounter
Than the instructive tale of *Godfrey the Geiger Counter.*

THE BIRTHDAY THAT NEVER WAS:
A FEBRUARY FANTASY

Washington, eighteen sixty-eight.
The night was cold, and the hour was late.
The dark Potomac, smooth as ice,
Mirrored the moon so you saw it twice —
But for once the moon was vanity-proof
And turned its face to the White House roof
Where the chimney smoke rose thin and slow
And told of a cherry-red hearth below.

The President lolled as much at ease
As he ever could, because of his knees
(Like his wrists and elbows, awkward points;
He seemed a creature composed of joints),
One hand ruffling his rebel hair,
And an arm along the arm of the chair;
Tranquillity his again, and mirth,
But he was the tiredest man on earth.

He raised his bearded chin from his breast
And thoughtfully spoke to the waiting guest:
I reckon you're stumped, Mr. Edwin Booth,
As to why you're here, so I'll tell the truth.

Your Brutus tonight had me overawed,
I was listening for Shakespeare to applaud;
But it's not to hang laurels on your brow,
Which must have more than enough by now;
The uncomplimentary fact remains
That I've taken a notion to pick your brains.
I've had reports from the politicians,
And ladies returning from earnest missions;
I know there are carpet-bagging cheaters
And unreconstructible ember-eaters,
Extremists ranting upon the scene —
But what of the millions in between?
You're just back from a tour of the South,
Give it me straight from the horse's mouth. . . .

Everywhere, sir, one tale to tell:
Below the Potomac all is well.

What of the wounds from the battle field?

A few still healing, but most are healed.
Thanks to a generous heart and hand
There is hope again in a stricken land.
They may be short of marble and gilding,
But with what they've got they are building.
You have proved that the Gray can blend with the Blue,
And bitterness fades like the summer dew.
A Southern lady, so help me Hannah,

Has married a Yankee in Savannah,
And if I may clinch my humble opinion,
There's talk that Texas approves the Union.

You bring, said the President, standing up,
Oil for my head and a brimming cup.
And thanks again for tonight's performance;
You made Brutus the noblest of murdering varmints.
— I'm a curious man who loves a sequel;
When will the stage present your equal?

Today there would be a finer and other,
John Wilkes Booth, my beloved brother;
But the yellow fever closed that door,
He died in Richmond in sixty-four.
But I talk too much when old memories stir;
Mr. Lincoln, a happy birthday, sir!

DETROIT, SPARE THAT WHEEL!

They who make automobiles,
They hate wheels.
They look on wheels as limbs were looked on by Victorian
aunts,
They conceal them in skirts and pants.
Wheels are as hard to descry as bluebirds in Lower Slobo-
via,
The only way you can see a wheel complete nowadays is
to look up at it while it is running ovia.
They who make automobiles,
They are ashamed of wheels,
Their minds are on higher things,
Their minds are on wings.
The concept of earthly vision is one that their designers
stray from;
Currently, a successful parking operation is one that you
can walk away from.
Unremittingly the manufacturers strive
To provide turnip-heads with cars that will do a hundred
and twenty miles an hour where the speed limit is
fifty-five.
The station wagon that shuttles the children between
home and school is hopelessly kaput

Unless two hundred and thirty horses are tugging at the accelerator under Mummy's foot.

I don't like wings, I like wheels;

I like automobiles.

I don't want to ride to the station or the office in jet-propelled planes,

All I want is a windshield wiper that really wipes the windshield, and some simple method of putting on chains.

CAESAR KNIFED AGAIN
or
CULTURE BIZ GETS HEP, BOFFS PROFS

To win the battle of life you have to plan strategical as
 well as tactical,
So I am glad that our colleges are finally getting practical.
If they're going to teach know-how
It's up to them to show how,
And one way to show it

Is to get rid of dead languages taught by professors who
are also dead but don't know enough to know it.
It's high time to rescue our kids from poetry and prunes
and prisms;
Once they start in on ideas and ideals they'll end up
spouting ideologies and isms.
Get them interested in hotel management and phys. ed.
and business administration instead of the so-called finer arts
And you'll cut off the flow of eggheads and do-gooders
and bleeding hearts.
Every campus gets what it deserves and deserves what it
gets,
So what do you want on yours — a lot of pinko longhairs,
or red-blooded athaletes and drum majorettes?
Another thing, now every autumn it's like the coach had
to open up a *new* factory,
But get rid of the classics and he can play his stars year
after year until they're ready for the glue factory,
Because they can never graduate, but no crowd of self-appointed reformers can raise a nasty aroma,
Because the reason they can never graduate is there won't
be anybody left who can write the Latin for their
diploma.
So now let's all go to the Victory Prom
And join in singing Alma Mom.

DO YOU PLAN TO SPEAK BANTU?
or
ABBREVIATION IS THE THIEF OF SANITY

The merchant, as crafty a man is he
As Haughton or Stagg or Zuppke;
He sells his wares by the broad turnpike,
Or, as some would have it, tpke.

The merchant offers us merchandise
Frozen or tinned or sudsy,
And the way that he spells his merchandise,
I have to pronounce it mdse.

'Twixt the wholesale price and the retail price
The merchant doth daily hustle,
His mdse he sells at the retail price,
But he buys his mdse whsle.

Let us purchase some whsle mdse, love,
And a shop will we set up
Where the turnpike runs through the township, love,
Where the tpke runs through the twp.

And you shall be as precious, love,
As a mermaidsk from Murmansk,
And I will tend the customers, love,
In a suit with two pr. pantsk.

HOW TO TELL A KITCHEN FROM A CUISINE: TAKE A QUICK LOOK AT OURS

Every time the menu lists *bleu* cheese I want to order *fromage* blue,
Don't you?
Yet when they call it *bleu* cheese I suppose they are right,
Because *bleu* cheese differs from blue cheese because it is usually white.
I must read up on this matter in the cheese cook book,
Which clutters up our kitchen along with the fish cook book, the game cook book, the wine cook book, the Colonial cook book, the French cook book, the Eskimo cook book and the Siamese cook book.
Yes, in our kitchen there are everywhere you look books,
There may be a stove, but you can't see the cook box for the cook books.
You know the way some larders are full of potatoes and lentils and beans?
That's the way ours is full of recipes clipped from newspapers and magazines.
Having perused this mass of culinariana I have one hope that is definite;
I hope we will always have a kitchen, but I hope I will never be the chef in it,
Because my few attempts to emulate Clementine Paddleford or Brillat-Savarin,

They have resulted in results something less than mouth-
waterin', or -slaverin'.
If there is one element of cookery I deplore,
It is that when you go to cook, the recipe suddenly calls
for a roux or a stock or something that should have
been started the day before.
I attribute the brilliance of Gian-Carlo Menotti
To the fact that he has never tasted my manicotti,
Because my ignorance is so profound
That I don't know whether manicotti should be rectangu-
lar or round.
In this respect even my limited knowledge of money is
preciser;
I know that the round kind is nice but the rectangular
kind is much nicer.

I CAN HARDLY WAIT FOR THE SANDMAN

There are several differences between me and Samuel Taylor Coleridge, whose bust I stand admiringly beneath;

He found solace in opium, I found it in Codman's Bayberry Chewing Gum — at least until it started loosening my teeth.

Another difference between me and Samuel Taylor Coleridge is more massive in design:

People used to interrupt him while he was dreaming his dreams, but they interrupt me while I am recounting mine.

Now, if anybody buttonholes you to tell you about how they dreamt they were falling, or flying, or just about to die and they actually would have died if they hadn't woken up abruptly,

Well, they deserve to be treated interruptly,

But when somebody with a really interesting dream takes the floor,

I don't think people ought to break away and start listening to the neighborhood bore.

Therefore I feel I need offer no apology

For having gathered a few of my more representative dreams into a modest anthology.

Once I dreamt I was in this sort of, you know, desert with cactuses only they were more like caterpillars and there were skulls and all the rest,

And right in the middle of this desert was a lifeboat with the name *Mary Celeste,*
And if I hadn't woken up because the heat was so blistery,
Why, I bet I would have solved this mystery of nautical history.
Another time I dreamt I was climbing this mountain although actually it was more like a beach,
And all of a sudden this sort of a merry-go-round I forgot to tell you about turned into a shack with a sign saying, LEDA'S PLACE, SWANBURGERS 10¢ EACH.
I hope you will agree that of dreams I am a connoisseur,
And next time I will tell you about either how I dreamt I went down the rabbit hole or through the looking glass, whichever you prefer.

IF FUN IS FUN, ISN'T THAT ENOUGH?

Child, the temptation please resist
To deify the humorist.
Simply because we're stuck with solons
Whose minds resemble lazy colons,
Do not assume our current jesters
Are therefore Solomons and Nestors.
Because the editorial column
Is ponderously trite and solemn
Don't think the wisdom of the ages
Awaits you in the comic pages.
There is no proof that Plato's brain
Weighed less than that of Swift or Twain.
If funny men are sometimes right
It's second guessing, not second sight;
They apply their caustic common sense
After, and not before, events.
Since human nature's a *fait accompli*
They puncture it regularly and promptly.
Some are sophisticates, some earthy,
And none are totally trustworthy;
They'll sell their birthright every time
To make a point or turn a rhyme.
This motto, child, is my bequest:
There's many a false word spoken in jest.

MR. BURGESS, MEET MR. BARMECIDE

Oft in the sleepless night I play a game that is of interest only to me:
I try to think of the character in fiction who I would rather not be.
Sometimes, when my mind is mussed,
I would rather not be Lear, or Tess, or Tony Last in *A Handful of Dust,*
But eventually one incontrovertible conclusion emerges,
I would most of all rather not be Yowler the Bobcat in the Nature stories of Thornton W. Burgess.
What with one generation and another, I have long been immersed in Nature stories up to my ears,
And so far as I know, unless someone pilfered an installment to wipe out an ashtray with, Yowler hasn't had a bite to eat in twenty years.
Just as he has Johnny Chuck set up neat as you please,
Why, Johnny Chuck is tipped off by a Merry Little Breeze.
Just as he has a clean shot at Jumper the Hare, who would do his system more good than a bucket of viosterol,
The same Merry Little Breeze tickles Jumper's sensitive nostril.
Currently, Yowler has his eye on the mouth-watering twins of Mrs. Lightfoot, an addlepated deer,

But he might just as well dehydrate his mouth and go
home; that Merry Little Breeze is frolicking near.
Now the author pauses to draw a character sketch of this
frustrated carnivorous rover;
And writes, "Fortunately for him he had long ago learned
to be patient," which to my mind is stating the case
under rather than over.
Patient, indeed!
I cry with Cassius, "Upon what meat doth this our Yowler
feed?"

MEL ALLEN, MEL ALLEN, LEND ME YOUR CLICHÉ

Let us sing of the unsung hero,
The pitcher too unrenowned,
Who is always in the bull pen,
But never reaches the mound.
It's 3 and 0 on the batter,
The bases are bursting full,
A 4-run lead has vanished,
And the manager signals the bull —
Yes, the manager signals the bull pen
To unlimber another bull.

There's MacTivity, MacTivity,
MacTivity in the bull pen!
He possesses every pitch in the book,
He's got the fast one, he's got the hook,
Slider, glider, sinker and knuckle,
MacTivity's master of many a muckle.
I know he's the lad to save the game,
But when they announce the reliefer's name
I can only guarantee that it's not
MacTivity, the talented Scot.
My hopes descend a deep declivity,
In the right field corner, there's MacTivity,
Subsiding in the bull pen.

He can throw from the port or starboard,
He's a regular pitching machine,
This wizard we all have heard of,
But no one has ever seen.
How the muscles bulge in his sweatshirt,
How his heart with hope is full,
When the manager beckons the bull pen
To send him another bull!
How he mutters a silent prayer,
Lord, let me be that bull!

There's MacTivity, MacTivity,
MacTivity in the bull pen!
And he doesn't warm up for only us,
MacTivity is ubiquitous,
MacTivity really gets around
For a pitcher who never reaches the mound.
Be it Baltimore, Brooklyn or Milwaukee,
There's MacTivity, posed and pawky.
Even in Mudville, when straits are dire
MacTivity's eager to quench the fire.
I know who I'd throw against Musial or Mantle,
But managers' minds are so infantile,
Managers' minds are flivverty-givverty,
In the right field corner, there's MacTivity,
Subsiding in the bull pen.

THE GREEKS HAD A WOID FOR IT, SO WHY SPEAK ENGLISH?

I know through intuition that Tereus was the son-in-law of King Pandion of Athens, and the eccentric husband of Procne,
But I know from experience that no Briton with any pretensions to culture can resist exhibiting his or her Cockney.
The more their brackets rise from middle to upper,
The less they can simply ask you for a simple meal and the more they have to go into the act and ask you for an ever so nice piece of 'addock and the inevitable nice 'ot cupper.
Some persons think this is pretty irritating insular jargon,
But I think that the British have themselves a typically tight little insular bargain,
Because they have only one dialect readily available to amateurs,
Whereas we have two, which is truly, if I may misuse a third dialect, calamiteuse.
This great country, which wants all its children to go to college but is distrustful of its adults with college degrees,
Why, it is also peopled with people who are convinced of their proficiency in speaking both Southern and Brooklynese.

As one who from the cradle obviously saw all and knew
all,
I early abandoned the hopeless fight against honey-chile
and you-all,
But I refuse to surrender to the other horror, which, if
we stand fast, we can avoid:
Namely, a lot of out-of-town jocose references to the corner of Toid Avenoo and Toity-toid.
I think I know from whence this reversion to the lingo of
Chimmie Fadden comes;
Its source is the inverted snobbery of a radio and TV audience that doesn't know anything about the Dodgers but loves to talk about Dem Bums.

I adore Pee Wee Reese and Carl Erskine, but I'm afraid
I detest non-Brooklynites to whom Oiskine is the
poil in their new-found erster,
And that's why I'm a Giants-firster.
Getting back to Tereus,
He married his wife's sister, Philomela, after telling her
that his wife, her sister Procne, was dead, subsequently cutting out Philomela's tongue and eating
his and Procne's child, after which they all got
changed into boids, and he took the woild serious.

THE TROUBLE WITH SHAKESPEARE, YOU REMEMBER HIM

I find it a sinecure to compile
My list of books for a desert isle.
Although of nests a feverish featherer,
I think ten books would be a plethora,
Of perilous and awkward bulk
To swim with from a sinking hulk,
So when I sight my island home
I'll salvage but a single tome,
Which is — what should it be, *sapristi,*
But any book by Agatha Christie?

I state without fear of successful bribery
One Christie book is as good as a libery.
By the time you close it, murmuring "Splendid!"
You've already forgotten how it ended.
The crime is baffling, the plot Promethean,
The solution is mixed with waters Lethean;
Whoever is fingered by Hercule Poirot
Is out of your head by this time tomorrow,
And the hundredth time you enter your Christiery
The same thick mist envelopes the mystery.
I repeat that one book by this murder-mongeress
Will last you as long as the Library of Congress.
Her full name is Agatha Christie Mallowan,
On my desert isle she is second to no one.

NEVER MIND THE OVERCOAT, BUTTON UP THAT LIP

Persons who have something to say like to talk about the arts and politics and economics,
And even the cultural aspects of the comics.
Among persons who have nothing to say the conversational content worsens;
They talk about other persons,
Sometimes they talk about persons they know personally, and rearrange their lives for them,
And sometimes they talk about persons they know through the tabloids, and rearrange their husbands and wives for them.
I have better things to talk about than fortune hunters who harry debs;
The causerie in my coterie is of how come Sir Arthur rewrote "The Red-headed League" under the title of "The Adventure of the Three Garridebs."
Gossip never darkens my doors
And I wouldn't trade one Gaboriau for a hatful of Gabors.
Do not praise me because to curious ears I will not pander,

I myself am not responsible for my abstention from libel and slander.
For this laudable trait there is a coony little old lady whom I am under obligation to;
She taught me that if you hear a juicy tidbit and don't repeat it within twenty-four hours, why, after that it is juiceless and there is no temptation to.
If you heed this precept you will never find yourself in a gossiper's role;
I know, because in 1915 when I discovered that Marie Jeanne Bécu Du Barry wasn't married to Louis XV I sat on the item for twenty-four hours and from that day till this I haven't breathed it to a living soul.

MY MY

I. MY DREAM

Here is a dream.
It is my dream —
My own dream —
I dreamt it.
I dreamt that my hair was kempt,
Then I dreamt that my true love unkempt it.

2. MY CONSCIENCE

I could of
If I would of,
But I shouldn't,
So I douldn't.

ME, I PLAY THE HARP, IT'S JUST ONE SYLLABLE

In my dealings with foreigners I have just one rule that
counts:
Live and let live, pronounce and let mispronounce.
Each race has its own linguistic customs,
And I see no reason to believe that ours are more rational
than Hiawatha's or Sohrab and Rustum's.
I hold that in Hindustan one should respect the culture
of the Hindu,
And when in Rome one should do as Shelley Winters and
Orson Welles and Errol Flynn do.
Just as it is natural for us to say "lobster," it is natural for
the French to say *langouste,*
And just as one of our Elder Statesmen might get
skunked at croquet, so the Maharajah of Maharaji-
pore might get mongoosed.
Abroad, I am linguistically open-minded,
But at home by prejudice I am blinded.
Therefore if to engage my good will thou plannest,
Please say pi*an*ist.
My leonine heart growls *Cœur de Li*onest
When people say *pi*anist.
You can get from the East to Ohio on either the C. 'n' O
or the B. 'n' O.,

But you can't be a *pi*anist unless you play on that non-existent instrument, a *pi*ano.
Have you heard of the famous *faux pas* that made Ward McAllister's cheeks glow the neonest?
His hostess, who already had everything, wished for one perfect peony, and he sent her Ignace Jan Paderewski, one perfect *pi*anist.

I CAN'T HAVE A MARTINI, DEAR, BUT YOU TAKE ONE

or

ARE YOU GOING TO SIT THERE GUZZLING ALL NIGHT?

Come, spread foam rubber on the floor,
And sawdust and excelsior;
Soundproof the ceiling and the wall,
Unwind the clock within the hall,
Muffle in cotton wool the knell
Of doorbell and of decibel.
Ye milkman and ye garbage man,
Clink not the bottle, clash not the can;
Ye census taker, pass on by,
And Fuller Brush man, draw not nigh;
Street cleaner, do not splash or sprinkle;
Good Humor man, forbear to tinkle;
Ye Communists, overt or crypto-,
Slink past this shuttered house on tiptoe,
And cat, before you seek admittance,
Put sneakers on yourself and kittens;
Let even congressmen fall quiet,
For Chloë is on her latest diet,
And when Chloë is straightening out her curves
She's a sensitive bundle of quivering nerves.

Me you will find it useless to quiz
On what her latest diet is,
So rapidly our Chloë passes
From bananas to wheat germ and molasses.
First she will eat but chops and cheese,
Next, only things that grow on trees,
Now buttermilk, now milk that's malted,
And saccharin, and salt de-salted,
Salads with mineral oil and lemon in,
Repugnant even to palates feminine,
Lean fish, and fowl as gaunt as avarice,
And haggard haggis and curds cadaverous.
Today may bring gluten bread and carrots,
Tomorrow the eggs of penguins or parrots,
Because Chloë's dietetic needs
Shift with each article she reads.
But whatever her diet, from whence or whither,
When Chloë's on it, there's no living with her.

I ALWAYS SAY THERE'S NO PLACE LIKE NEW YORK IN THE SUMMER

or

THAT COTTAGE SMALL BY A WATERFALL WAS SNAPPED UP LAST FEBRUARY

Estivation means passing the summer in a torpid condition, which is why I love to estivate,
But I find that planning my estivation is as chaotic as the nightmares caused by that fried lobster with garlic sauce which I when restive and indigestive ate.
When icicles hang by the wall and people smear Chap Stick on their faces
I can't seem to take it in that the hounds of Spring are actually on Winter's traces.
The subfreezing months are what my wits are frozen and subhuman in;
Sing cuccu never so lhude, cuccu cannot convince me that Sumer is icumen in.
Consequently, on my Sumer plans I do not embark
Until the first crocus has ventured into Central Park.
But come the first crocus,
You can't locate a desirable Sumer location even with the aid of abracadabra, open sesame, hanky panky and hocus pocus.
By the time you start pleading with rural realtors estival,

Why, they have had themselves a financial festival.
Be it seaside or lakeside, they have rented every habitable tent and bungalow,
Presumably to foresighted tenants who must have stood in line since the days of Jean Ingelow or even Michelangelo.
The only properties left are such as were despised by Thoreau before he departed for Walden,
With President Pierce plumbing and the kind of lighting under which Priscilla almost got Miles Standish mixed up with John Alden.
This coming Sumer I must remind myself to remember
That the time to arrange for the Sumer after this is before this coming September.
Meanwhile I guess I'll just sit in the city sipping gin and tonics,
Nibbling those tasty garden-fresh vegetables raised in a twelfth-floor dining alcove by hydroponics.

UP FROM THE EGG:
THE CONFESSIONS OF A NUTHATCH AVOIDER

Bird watchers top my honors list.
I aimed to be one, but I missed.
Since I'm both myopic and astigmatic,
My aim turned out to be erratic,
And I, bespectacled and binocular,
Exposed myself to comment jocular.
We don't need too much birdlore, do we,
To tell a flamingo from a towhee;
Yet I cannot, and never will,
Unless the silly birds stand still.

And there's no enlightenment in a tour
Of ornithological literature.
Is yon strange creature a common chickadee,
Or a migrant *alouette* from Picardy?
You rush to consult your Nature guide
And inspect the gallery inside,
But a bird in the open never looks
Like its picture in the birdie books —
Or if it once did, it has changed its plumage,
And plunges you back into ignorant gloomage.
That is why I sit here growing old by inches,
Watching the clock instead of finches,
But I sometimes visualize in my gin
The Audubon that I audubin.

I KNOW EXACTLY WHO DROPPED THE OVERALLS IN MRS. MURPHY'S CHOWDER

I know a man named Mr. Nagle.
He is what the Scots call a wallydraigle.
A wallydraigle is a weak underdeveloped creature, sometimes the last-born of a litter,
And I can think of no description fitter.
You'd never know Mr. Nagle was there
If he weren't in your hair.
His collar is never quite in touch with his neck,
And he drops in on Sunday afternoon to ask if you can cash a small check.

He makes a beeline for that antique gilt chair with the
wobbly leg,
And leans back in it creakily and anteakily while feeding
pretzels and popcorn to the dog which you have just
finished training not to beg.
His anecdotes are proof that he believes it better to travel
hopefully than to arrive,
And when he tosses his chewing-gum wrappers at the
wastebasket, he hits it three times out of five.
The economics of housewifery are beyond his scope;
After he has washed his hands, you find he has used
three fresh towels and two new cakes of soap.
Yes, Mr. Nagle is the housewife's pet.
He can mess up half a dozen clean ash trays with one
regular-size cigarette.
Sometimes he goes to the opposite pole,
He puts dead matches back in the matchbox, and cracks
nuts and puts the shells back in the bowl.
No matter how deeply you are planted in a peaceful day
at home, Mr. Nagle can uproot you;
Scots wha' hae wi' wallydraigles bled, I salute you.

ATTITUDES TOWARD GRATITUDE FROM SELECTIONS FROM EARLY RECOLLECTIONS

Now that what were once to me modern days have become olden
My memories get more and more golden.
I think of everybody to whom I was in my youth beholden,
And gratitude does my pen embolden.

I am grateful to my old nurse who did me awaken to see Halley's comet
And told me to turn my head away when my little brother did vomit,
And particular gratitude to my parents I have sworn
Because without their aid I could not have been born.

I am grateful to all my teachers, whether they dwelt in a hut or a palace,
Because their lore did light up my zenith like the aurora borealis.
They may have used a stick of hickory
But they taught me much culture and history.

I am grateful for the innocent days of childhood,
Whether on city pavements or out in the wildwood,
Albeit that though playing Halma or football
Always at my back I did hear Time's footfall.

So I promised myself that when I grew to manhood
I would never forget the friends of my youth like old
canned goods.
Cynics may claim that gratitude is a catastrophe,
But let us hope that gratitude will never atrophy.

OLD IS FOR BOOKS

A poet named Robert Browning eloped with a poetess
named Elizabeth Barrett,
And since he had an independent income they lived in an
Italian villa instead of a London garret.
He created quite a furor
With his elusive caesura.
He also created a youthful sage,
A certain Rabbi Ben Ezra who urged people to hurry up
and age.
This fledgling said, Grow old along with me,
The best is yet to be.
I term him fledgling because such a statement, certes,
Could emanate only from a youngster in his thirties.
I have a friend named Ben Azzara who is far from a
fledgling,

Indeed he is more like from the bottom of the sea of life
a barnacled dredgling.
He tells me that as the years have slipped by
He has become utterly dependent on his wife because he
has forgotten how to tie his tie.
He says he sleeps after luncheon instead of at night,
And he hates to face his shaving mirror because although
his remaining hair is brown his moustache comes
out red and his beard comes out white.
Furthermore, he says that last week he was stranded for
thirty-six hours in his club
Because he couldn't get out of the tub.
He says he was miserable, but when he reflected that the
same thing probably eventually happened to Rabbi
Ben Ezra
It relieved his mizra.

PERIOD PERIOD

PERIOD I

Our fathers claimed, by obvious madness moved,
Man's innocent until his guilt is proved.
They would have known, had they not been confused,
He's innocent until he is accused.

PERIOD II

The catch phrase "Nothing human to me is alien"
Was coined by some South European rapscallion.
This dangerous fallacy I shall now illumine:
To chauvinists, nothing alien is human.

IF I HAD THE WINGS OF A HELIOCOPTER
or
HALL'S MILLS THAT ENDS MILLS

Some people bet against Native Dancer,
And other people ask questions and don't wait to listen to
the answer.
To treat them with patience requires special training;
They ask you if it's raining and you say Yes and they go
out without an umbrella and get wet and say why
didn't you tell them it was raining.
They ask you if you had any interesting experiences when
you were lost on Mount Everest
And before you can say "abominable snowman" they tell
you that maybe Jackie Gleason is the funniest but
Milton Berle is the cleverest.
Eyes have they and see not, and ears and hear not,
And inaccuracy they fear not.
I guess whoever taught them to read
Didn't quite succeed.
I can control my chills
When in discussing murder cases they refer to the Halls-
Mills,
But in my heart there is no charity
When they speak of the struggle between Holmes and
Professor Moriarity.

Children dear, let us away from such fuzzy-mindedness,
as Dorothy Arnold wrote in "The Forsaken Merman,"
Let us away to the graduation ceremonies at Duke University and listen to the tobaccalaureate sermon.

NO WOE IS GOSSAMER TO MR. BESSEMER

Perhaps Mr. Bessemer is not a pessimist but, last and
first,
He expects the worst.
It could be aptly put
That Mr. Bessemer got out of the cradle on the wrong
foot.
He suspects that any dish prepared outside the home and
many prepared inside the home will break him out
in purple spots and red spots,

And that the Federal Communications Commission anticipates where he is going to place his radio and TV and rushes ahead to fill his air with dead spots;
He is certain that the train he must catch will leave early, and that, once caught, it will arrive late,
And, as a Michigan alumnus, that the Big Ten title will go to Ohio State.
But it is on the subject of the weather
That his forebodings really get together.
Mr. Bessemer is the holidaymakers' bane;
His ears are filled with ancestral voices prophesying rain.
Be the sunset garish as a festival in Spain,
Mr. Bessemer predicts rain;
Be the sunrise cheery as Mr. Wodehouse's fiction,
Rain is his prediction;
While if on the eve of a three-day week end the skies be runny,
He conjures up a northeaster; in fact, some people call him the North Easter bunny.
Yes, Mr. Bessemer has predicted rain under all circumstances except one,
And that was during a drought in Texas, and a big cloud came up, and he predicted sun.

THE INVITATION SAYS FROM FIVE TO SEVEN

There's nothing like an endless party,
A collection of clammy little groups,
Where a couple of the guests are arty
And the rest of the guests are goops.
There's the confidential girlish chatter —
It soothes you like a drug —
And the gentle pitter-patter
As the anchovies hit the rug.
There's the drip, drip, drip of the mayonnaise
As the customers slither through the canapés,
There are feuds that are born,
There are friendships that pine away,
And the big cigar that smolders on the Steinaway.
The major trouble with a party
Is you need a guest to give it for,
And the best part of any guest
Is the last part out the door.

There's nothing like an endless party,
And there hasn't been since ancient Rome.
Here's Silenus making passes at Astarte
While Mrs. Silenus begs him to go home.
There is bigamy about the boudoirs,
There is bundling at the bar,

And the sideboard where the food was
Has the aspect of an abattoir.
You wonder why they pursue each other's wives,
Who by now resemble the cream cheese and the chives.
There's a corpse on the floor
From New Rochelle or Scarborough,
And its mate is swinging from the candelabara.
The best location for a party
Is in a room without a floor,
And the best way to give a party
Is leave town the night before.

I'LL EAT MY SPLIT-LEVEL TURKEY IN THE BREEZEWAY

A lady I know disapproves of the vulgarization of Christmas; she believes that Christmas should be governed purely by spiritual and romantic laws;
She says all she wants for Christmas is no more suggestive songs about Santa Claus.
Myself, I am more greedy if less cuddle-y,
And being of '02 vintage I am perforce greedy fuddy-duddily,
So my own Christmas could be made glad
Less by the donation of anything new than just by the return of a few things I once had.
Some people strive for gracious living;
I have recurrent dreams of spacious living.
Not that I believe retrogression to be the be-all and the end-all,
Not that I wish to spend the holidays sitting in a Turkish corner smoking Sweet Caps and reading *Le Rouge et le Noir* by Stendhal,
Nor do I long for a castle with machicolations,
But I would like a house with a porte-cochere so the guests wouldn't get wet if it rained the evening of my party for my rich relations.
Also, instead of an alcove I'd like a dining room that there wasn't any doubt of,

And a bathtub that you didn't have to send $7.98 to Wisconsin for a device that enables you to hoist yourself out of,
And if there is one thought at which every cockle of my heart perks up and warms,
It is that of an attic in which to pile old toys and magazines and fancy dress costumes and suitcases with the handle off and dressmaker's forms.
I'd like a house full of closets full of shelves,
And above all, a house with lots of rooms all with doors that shut so that every member of the family could get off alone by themselves.
Please find me such a relic, dear Santa Claus, and when you've done it,
Please find me an old-fashioned cook and four old-fashioned maids at $8.00 a week and a genial wizard of a handyman to run it.

THE SELF-EFFACEMENT OF ELECTRA THORNE

Everybody knows who is the greatest actress ever born;
Why, if you rolled the Misses Hayes and Cornell into one and tripled them, you would only begin to approximate Electra Thorne.
Some call Electra Thorne ill-tempered because when her dear old mother let her go on with her slip showing she kicked her dear old mother in the breeks,
But gosh, everybody around the theater had been wanting to do that for weeks.

It seems unfair to call her prone to temperamental rage
Simply because she insisted on the firing of an elderly bit player because he reminded her of her father, whose financial failure forced her out of Sarah Lawrence onto the stage.
As for egocentricity, good heavens!
What's egocentric about wanting the marquee to read

ELECTRA THORNE
IN
OPHELIA AND HAMLET
WITH
MAURICE EVANS
?

Yet on their honeymoon there was some trepidation in the mind of Hoover Grimalkin, her groom;
He was wondering how to register for the room.
He was a writer who had won three Pulitzer Prizes, two Critics' Awards and an Oscar,
And he was at work on the libretto of a bebop version of *Tosca.*
His bride had assured him that she did not wish her career to intrude upon their private life,
He was the artist in the family, she said, and her only desire was to be a common, ordinary, everyday, just plain wife.
But Mr. Grimalkin had not been totally unobservant during his wooing;
He had a distinct feeling: no billing, no cooing.

So, thinking quickly, he asked Electra to register, he said his handwriting was a disgrace.
And she registered as "Mrs. Hoover Grimalkin and husband," and now he walks her poodle every day in Sutton Place.

THE SNARK WAS A BOOJUM WAS A PRAWN

A giant new prawn has been dredged up near Santiago, Chile . . . it is succulent and mysterious. . . . The new prawn has not been named, a fact that is causing no concern in Chile.

— TIMES

Could some descending escalator
Deposit me below the equator,
I'd hunt me a quiet Chilean haunt,
Some Santiago restaurant;
The fact I speak no *Español*
Would handicap me not at all,
Since any language would be aimless
In ordering a tidbit nameless;
I'd simply tie my napkin on
And gesture like a giant prawn,
Then, served the dish for which I yearned,
Proceed to munch it, unconcerned.
Happy crustacean, anonymous prawn,
From distant Latin waters drawn,
Hadst thou in Yankee seas appeared,
Account executives would have cheered,
Vice-presidents in paroxysms
Accorded thee multiple baptisms;
Yea, shouldst thou hit our markets now,
Soon, prawn, wouldst thou be named — and how!

I see the bright ideas drawn:
Prawno, Prawnex, and Vitaprawn;
And, should upper-bracket dreamers wake,
Squab o' Neptune, and Plankton Steak.
Small wonder thou headest for Santiago,
Where gourmets ignore such frantic farrago;
That's exactly where I myself would have went if I'd
Been mysterious, succulent, unidentified.

THERE'LL ALWAYS BE A WAR BETWEEN THE SEXES

or

A WOMAN CAN BE SOMETIMES PLEASED, BUT NEVER SATISFIED

I used to know a breadwinner named Mr. Purefoy who
was far from the top of the heap,

Indeed he could only be called a breadwinner because he had once won half a loaf of whole wheat in the Irish Sweep.
His ambition was feverish,
His industry was eager-beaverish,
His wife was a thrifty helpmeet who got full value for every disbursement,
Yet their financial status showed no betterment, just perpetual worsement.
The trouble with these two was that they dissipated their energies,
They didn't play the percenages.
If he got angry at a slovenly, insolent waiter when they were dining in town
She would either bury her face in the menu or try to calm him down.
If she got angry at the woman in front of her at the movies and loudly suggested that she push her hat a little lower,
He pretended he didn't know her.
He defended his unappreciative employer against her loyal wifely ire,
And when he got burned up about the bills from the friendly exorbitant little grocer around the corner she tried to put out the fire.
One day they had a thought sublime,
They thought, Let's both get mad at the same person or situation at the same time.
I don't know about Mars, but Earth has not a denizen,

Who can withstand the wrath of a husband and wife being wrathful in unison.
To be said, little remains;
Only that after they merged their irascibility, it required the full time of three Certified Public Accountants and one Certified Private Accountant to keep track of their capital gains.

PREFACE TO THE PAST

Time all of a sudden tightens the tether,
And the outspread years are drawn together.
How confusing the beams from memory's lamp are;
One day a bachelor, the next a grampa.
What is the secret of the trick?

How did I get so old so quick?
Perhaps I can find by consulting the files
How step after step added up to miles.
I was sauntering along, my business minding,
When suddenly struck by affection blinding,

Which led to my being a parent nervous
Before they invented the diaper service.
I found myself in a novel pose,
Counting infant fingers and toes.
I tried to be as wise as Diogenes
In the rearing of my two little progenies,
But just as I hit upon wisdom's essence
They changed from infants to adolescents.
I stood my ground, being fairly sure
That one of these days they must mature,

So when I was properly humbled and harried,
They did mature, and immediately married.
Now I'm counting, the cycle being complete,
The toes on my children's children's feet.
Here lies my past, good-by I have kissed it;
Thank you, kids, I wouldn't have missed it.

THE STRANGE CASE OF THE LUCRATIVE COMPROMISE

Some people are in favor of compromising, while other people to compromise are loath.
I cannot plump for either side, I think there is something to be said for both.
But enough of discussion, let us proceed to example,
Of which the experience of Porteous Burnham should be ample.
The infant Burnham was a prodigious phenomenon, a phenomenon truly prodigious,
His parents and teachers regarded him with awe verging on the religious.
His genius was twofold, it appeared to have no ceiling,
And it was directed toward the science of lexicography and the science of healing.
Anatomy and etymology were Pablum to the infant Burnham;
At the age of five he knew that people don't sit down on their sternum,
Although he would occasionally say so in jest,
Later explaining that the word derived from the Greek *sternon,* meaning chest.
At the age of twenty-one he was an M.D. and a D. Litt., but his career hung in the balance,

Because he couldn't choose between his talents,
Until one day he was approached by an advertising agency that had heard of his dual gift,
And to work out a compromise they made shift,
And now he is the one who thinks up those frightening pseudo-scientific names for all the strange new ailments the consumer gets —
That is, if he uses some other sponsor's toothpaste or cigarettes;
And he makes a hundred thousand dollars a year, U.S. not Mexican,
Because the compromise landed him in a luxurious penthouse on Park Avenue, which is midway between Medicine and Lexicon.

THE STRANGE CASE OF THE BLIGHT THAT FAILED

or

NEVER UNDERESTIMATE THE POWER OF A GREAT-AUNT

If anybody is listening,
I want to talk about the happy outcome of a disastrous
    christening.
The parents not only named the baby Hieronymus,
They also forgot to invite his malevolent great-aunt, Mrs.
    Spuyten Duyvil Verplanck, who in this narrative
    shall remain anonymous,
And she vented her wrath on the child, poor lambie,
And he grew up under the burden of a multiple whammy.

He always ordered pineapple juice, which he detested,
because he was afraid to say tomahto juice to waitresses,
Because they would have corrected his pronunciation because all waitresses are tomaitresses.
At sight of his luxurious wall-to-wall carpeting, his friends would vociferously enthuse,
And then leave their puppies with him when they went on a Caribbean cruise.
If a telephoned order for a dozen hamburgers with relish and a ham and cheese on rye interrupted his slumber,
He apologized for being the wrong number.
His apartment was at ground level, although into a penthouse he would have loved to soar,
Because he couldn't sustain a conversation with elevator operators beyond the second floor.
Thanks to his wicked great-aunt, Hieronymus was a meek and diffident mouse which the whole world had its foot upon,
He was wasting away from being constantly put upon,
But when he was down to ninety-eight pounds his *good* great-aunt sent him a case of wet heavy beer and now he is over two hundred, and headwaiters and beautiful women are to him but toys,
And all because of his belated weighty presence, or overdue poise.

A TALE OF THE THIRTEENTH FLOOR

The hands of the clock were reaching high
In an old midtown hotel;
I name no name, but its sordid fame
Is table talk in hell.
I name no name, but hell's own flame
Illumes the lobby garish,
A gilded snare just off Times Square
For the maidens of the parish.

The revolving door swept the grimy floor
Like a crinoline grotesque,
And a lowly bum from an ancient slum
Crept furtively past the desk.
His footsteps sift into the lift
As a knife in the sheath is slipped,
Stealthy and swift into the lift
As a vampire into a crypt.

Old Maxie, the elevator boy,
Was reading an ode by Shelley,
But he dropped the ode as it were a toad
When the gun jammed into his belly.
There came a whisper as soft as mud
In the bed of an old canal:

"Take me up to the suite of Pinball Pete,
The rat who betrayed my gal."

The lift doth rise with groans and sighs
Like a duchess for the waltz,
Then in middle shaft, like a duchess daft,
It changes its mind and halts.
The bum bites lip as the landlocked ship
Doth neither fall nor rise,
But Maxie the elevator boy
Regards him with burning eyes.
"First, to explore the thirteenth floor,"
Says Maxie, "would be wise."

Quoth the bum, "There is moss on your double cross,
I have been this way before,
I have cased the joint at every point,
And there is no thirteenth floor.
The architect he skipped direct
From twelve unto fourteen,
There is twelve below and fourteen above,
And nothing in between,
For the vermin who dwell in this hotel
Could never abide thirteen."

Said Max, "Thirteen, that floor obscene,
Is hidden from human sight;
But once a year it doth appear,
On this Walpurgis Night.

Ere you peril your soul in murderer's role,
Heed those who sinned of yore;
The path they trod led away from God,
And onto the thirteenth floor,
Where those they slew, a grisly crew,
Reproach them forevermore.

"We are higher than twelve and below fourteen,"
Said Maxie to the bum,
"And the sickening draft that taints the shaft
Is a whiff of kingdom come.
The sickening draft that taints the shaft
Blows through the devil's door!"
And he squashed the latch like a fungus patch,
And revealed the thirteenth floor.

It was cheap cigars like lurid scars
That glowed in the rancid gloom,
The murk was a-boil with fusel oil
And the reek of stale perfume.
And round and round there dragged and wound
A loathsome conga chain,
The square and the hep in slow lock step,
The slayer and the slain.
(For the souls of the victims ascend on high,
But their bodies below remain.)

The clean souls fly to their home in the sky,
But their bodies remain below

To pursue the Cain who each has slain
And harry him to and fro.
When life is extinct each corpse is linked
To its gibbering murderer,
As a chicken is bound with wire around
The neck of a killer cur.

Handcuffed to Hate come Doctor Waite
(*He* tastes the poison now),
And Ruth and Judd and a head of blood
With horns upon its brow.
Up sashays Nan with her feathery fan
From *Floradora* bright;
She never hung for Caesar Young,
But she's dancing with him tonight.

Here's the bulging hip and the foam-flecked lip
Of the mad dog, Vincent Coll,
And over there that ill-met pair,
Becker and Rosenthal.
Here's Legs and Dutch and a dozen such
Of braggart bullies and brutes,
And each one bends 'neath the weight of friends
Who are wearing concrete suits.

Now the damned make way for the double-damned
Who emerge with shuffling pace
From the nightmare zone of persons unknown,
With neither name nor face.

And poor Dot King to one doth cling,
Joined in a ghastly jig,
While Elwell doth jape at a goblin shape
And tickle it with his wig.

See Rothstein pass like breath on a glass,
The original Black Sox kid;
He riffles the pack, riding piggyback
On the killer whose name he hid.
And smeared like brine on a slavering swine,
Starr Faithful, once so fair,
Drawn from the sea to her debauchee,
With the salt sand in her hair.

And still they come, and from the bum
The icy sweat doth spray;
His white lips scream as in a dream,
"For God's sake, let's away!
If ever I meet with Pinball Pete
I will not seek his gore,
Lest a treadmill grim I must trudge with him
On the hideous thirteenth floor."

"For you I rejoice," said Maxie's voice,
"And I bid you go in peace,
But I am late for a dancing date
That nevermore will cease.
So remember, friend, as your way you wend,
That it would have happened to you,

But *I* turned the heat on Pinball Pete;
You see — *I* had a daughter, too!"

The bum reached out and he tried to shout,
But the door in his face was slammed,
And silent as stone he rode down alone
From the floor of the double-damned.

THE STRANGE CASE OF MR. WOOD'S FRUSTRATION

or

A TEAM THAT WON'T BE BEATEN BETTER STAY OFF THE FIELD

Once there was a man named Mr. Culpepper Wood,
And for him the best was none too good.
Unfortunately, he never got to get the best;
While somebody else was walking off with it, he was still
looking for it with the rest.
When he got his name on the cup,
It was always as runner-up.

Nobody than he was kithier and kinnier,
But he came from one of the second families of Virginia.
His character was without a smirch,
But it never got him further than the Second Presbyterian
Church.
He was of high financial rank,
But his account landed in the Second National Bank.
He finally realized he hadn't made the grade
When he was knocked down by a repossessed scooter and
the Boy Scouts administered Second Aid.
It was then that he allowed that he reckoned
That he was tired of being second.
He took an advanced course in baby talk at a progressive
university,
After which he spent three days in the desert without
even a mirage to sip, and cried triumphantly, "Now
me firsty."

TABLE TALK

1. YORKSHIRE PUDDING

Let us call Yorkshire pudding
A fortunate blunder;
It's a sort of popover
That tripped and popped under.

2. THE SWEETBREAD

That sweetbread gazing up at me
Is not what it purports to be.
Says Webster in one paragraph,
It is the pancreas of a calf.
Since it is neither sweet nor bread,
I think I'll take a bun instead.

3. THE PIZZA

Look at itsy-bitsy Mitzi!
See her figure slim and ritzy!
She eatsa
Pizza!
Greedy Mitzi!
She no longer itsy-bitsy!

4. THE SHAD

I'm sure that Europe never had
A fish as tasty as the shad.
Some people greet the shad with groans,
Complaining of its countless bones;
I claim the bones teach table poise
And separate the men from boys.
The shad must be dissected subtle-y;
Besides, the roe is boneless, utterly.

TO EE IS HUMAN

Once there were two men named Mr. Webster and Mr. Merriam,
And they had many differences but in the face of a common danger they decided to bury 'em.
Some people, vouchsafed Mr. Webster, can't see the wood for the trees,
But I can't see the language for the rising tide of double e's.
I know, vouched Mr. Merriam even more safely, that jargon will someday overwhelm our mother tongue, but I can remember before it had begun to,
And the suffix *er* denoted who did it and suffix *ee* denoted who it was done to.
In my day, barked Mr. Webster, an employer employed an employee, and a trustee was one who was trusted.
Which, bowwowed Mr. Merriam, although beside the point, is why many trusters went busted.
Who, rapped Mr. Webster, escapes an escapee?
That, knock-knocked Mr. Merriam, is what puzzles me.
Has the moment come, rapiered Mr. Webster, to abjectly surrender to journalese?
On that, riposted Mr. Merriam, you may bet not only your shirt but also your jacket and trousees.

Well, epitaphed Mr. Webster, none so blind as those who
will not see;
In the future please address me not as Mr. Webster but
as Mr. Webstee.

THAT'S FUNNY, WASN'T IT? NO, IT WON'T BE

Stranger, ignore yon loud bassoon
And harken, ere thou departest,
To the plaintive notes of a minor tune,

The wail of the comic artist.
The shadows lengthen across his career,
Each day is a new conundrum,
As the wingèd horses of yesteryear
Are progressively shot from under him.

His predecessors had ready themes,
Dependable sturdy stanchions,
And never foresaw in their direst dreams
The birth of a social conscience.
A permanent company they employed
Of dramatis personae;
There were Abie and Ike, and Pat and Mike,
And Rastus, Ole, and Tony.

But the humor that once raised mirthful whoops
Grew more and more precarious;
The facetious baiting of minor groups
Seemed less and less hilarious.
So the artist discarded the racial joke
And packed it away in camphor,
And assembled a group of risible folk
That nobody gives a damn for.

There's the couple marooned on the desert isle
With a caption faintly risqué,
And the portly sultan with lecherous smile
And entourage odalisqué,
The fakir complete with his bag of tricks,

The witch doctor, his cousin-german,
The felon reviewing his awkward fix,
And the khan on the flying Kirman.

So far, so good, but the world is filled
With sensitive True Believers,
There may come a complaint from the Sultans' Guild
Or the Magic Carpet Weavers.
How long can the ink-stained wretch rely
On his file of new sidesplitters
In the face of a logical outraged cry
From the Union of Counterfeiters?

Stranger, the wedding feast is done,
But linger, ere thou departest,
To murmur a prayer, just a little one,
For the soul of the comic artist.
May he sit secure on a laughing star
And cartoon on heavenly ceilings
The saints, who so superior are
That nothing can hurt their feelings.

WHAT'S IN A NAME? HERE'S WHAT'S IN A NAME

or

I WONDER WHAT BECAME OF JOHN AND MARY

In movies I prefer something unpretentious, like "Marty,"
But who wants an unpretentious party?
I always say a nice, pretentious party will do more for
your ego than doctors or medicine;
I wish you could have been at the one I tossed recently to
celebrate the payment of my bill from Con Edison.
There was Cary Middlecoff, Carey Latimer, Cary Grant,
Gary Cooper, Gary Crosby, and, I think but I'm
not quite sure,
Garry Moore.
Also Rocky Marciano, Rocky Graziano, Rocky Castellani,
Rock Hudson, and, showing great endurance,
A man from Prudential Insurance.
I don't want to talk your ear off,
But I mustn't forget Kim Stanley, Kim Hunter, Kim No-
vak, and Akim Tamiroff;
An added entry
Was Speed Lamkin and Race Gentry;
And guess who crowded together hotly discussing Scho-
penhauer and Nietzsche —
Donna Atwood, Donna Reed, and Don Ameche!

And who up for the conga should line
But Julie Andrews, Julie Wilson, Julie Harris, Julie Haydon, Julie Adams, and Jule Styne!
It was such a pretentious party that all my vapors did disappear.
I also had Katie and Audrey just to prove that it can Hepburn here.

TRY IT SUNS. AND HOLS.; IT'S CLOSED THEN

I know a little restaurant
Behind a brownstone stoop
Where *potage du jour* is French
For a can of onion soup.

You order a Martini without an olive in it;
They bring you a Martini, it has an olive in it.
Throw the olive on the floor,
That's what the floor is for.

The tables teem with ladies
Tuned up by Mistress Arden,
And Muzak fills the air
With "In a Persian Garden."

You order legs of frog, and please omit the garlic;
They bring you legs of frog, all redolent of garlic.
Throw the frogs' legs on the floor,
That's what the floor is for.

The Daiquiris are flowing
Before the meal and after;
The smoke from fifty filter tips
Is shaken by the Schraffter.

You ask them for an ash tray, a receptacle for ashes;
They do not bring an ash tray, instead they bring a menu.
Throw the ashes on the floor,
That's what the floor is for.

I know a little restaurant
Where client and agent grapple,
Where *ananas au kirsch*
Is French for canned pineapple.

You ask them for the check, for *l'addition,* for the bill;
They do not bring the check, they bring another menu.
Throw the menu on the floor,
Walk quickly through the door,
That's what the door is for.

POSIES FROM A SECOND CHILDHOOD
or
HARK HOW GAFFER DO CHAFFER

1. DADDY'S HOME, SEE YOU TOMORROW

I always found my daughters' beaux
Invisible as the emperor's clothes,
And I could hear of them no more
Than the slamming of an auto door.
My chicks would then slip up to roost;
They were, I finally deduced,
Concealing tactfully, pro tem,
Not boys from me but me from them.

2. THE ABSENTEES

The healthy human child will keep
Away from home, except to sleep.
Were it not for the common cold,
Our young we never would behold.

3. A BOY'S WILL IS THE WIND'S WILL?

Mr. Longfellow spoke only part of the truth,
Though a fatherly poet of pre-eminent rank;
A girl's will is the twister's will.
It can drive a parent through a two-inch plank.

HOW TO HARRY A HUSBAND
or
IS THAT ACCESSORY REALLY NECESSARY?

Husband stands at door of flat,
Coat in elbow, hand on hat,
In his pocket, from broker shady,
Two good seats for *My Fair Lady*.
Patiently he stands there humming,
Coming, darling? Darling, coming?

But she's a freak and she's a hag,
She's got the wrong, she murmurs, bag,
She's got, she adds in wild distress,
To change the bag or change the dress.
She'd as soon appear with stockings ragged
As be seen incongruously bebaggèd.

Husband rings the bell for lift,
Hears it chunk and upward drift,
Well knows taxis in the rain
Rarer than the whooping crane.
Impatiently he stands there snarling,
Darling, coming? Coming, darling?

Another bag at last she chooses
And everything in the first bag loses.
She fumbles with many a dainty curse
For lipstick, glasses, keys, and purse.*
He grunts, as dies preprandial liquor,
To change from the skin out would have been quicker.

They disrupt the middle of the show,
Their seats are middle of the row,
They crawl and climb like tandem tractors
Between the audience and the actors,
Whose delicious rapport might have lagged
Had she been incongruously bebagged.

* Then —
She turns it inside out and scratches
For handkerchief, cigarettes, and matches,
Tweezers, compact, and aspirin,
And Band-Aids redolent of My Sin,
Driver's license and Charga-Plate,
A sweepstake ticket one year late,
A colored chart of a five-day diet,
A Penguin commended by Gilbert Highet,
A tearful appeal from a charitymonger,
And a catalogue from Lewis & Conger.
This is she whose eyes start from their sockets
At the contents of her small son's pockets.

RAPUNZEL, RAPUNZEL, LET'S LET DOWN OUR HAIR

Once there was a fair young damsel and she early went,
from an inferiority complex, out of her wits,
Because her friends at Wolfcroft were Miss Diana Fitz-James, Miss Perdita Fitz-Clarence, and the Honorable Miss Mavis Fitz-Something-or-other, and she herself was only Miss Rapunzel Fitts.
Rapunzel went around singing that mares and does won't eat ivy, but little lambs 'll,
So she was really more a dumsel than a damsel.
She had another song for festive occasions, when none was so festive as she;

She sang "Marilyn Monrollalong o'er the Debussy."
She was a joy to behold, but her mind worked clumsily,
Or, shall we say, dumsily.
After three semesters of *Hamlet* she still couldn't tell handsaws from hawks,
And she thought the Gunpowder Plot involved poisoning the Parliament with toadstools because she had learned on a nature-walk that fungus was made before Fawkes.
In a Scandinavian fjord where she visited her friend Miss Fjitz-ffjoulkes on a rocky islet
She responded, when asked if her brother in the Air Force was a pilot yet, No, he's a yet pilot.
The last I heard of her, she had married a realtor, name of Babbitt,
And she was at a dinner with her mind on green peas, sitting beside another realtor who said, I'm from Cedar Rapids, and she thought he said, I'm Peter Rabbit.
This episode was on Rapunzel's memory permanently etched,
And she has grown old wondering whether he really was Peter Rabbit, or whether he was just a little bit tetched.

WHAT, NO SHEEP?

WHAT, NO SHEEP? These are a few of the 600 products sold in the "sleep shop" of a New York department store.

— *From an advertisement of the Consolidated Edison Company in the* TIMES

I don't need no sleepin' medicine —
I seen a ad by ole Con Edison.
Now when I lay me on my mattress
You kin hear me snore from hell to Hatteras,
With muh Sleep Record,
Muh Vaporizer,
Muh Electric Slippers,
Muh Yawn Plaque,
Muh Slumber Buzzer,
Muh miniature Electric Organ,
An' muh wonderful Electric Blanket.

My old woman couldn't eat her hominy —
Too wore out from the durned insominy.
She give insominy quite a larrupin',
Sleeps like a hibernatin' tarrapin,
With her Eye Shade,
Her Clock-Radio,
Her Sinus Mask,
Her Massagin' Pillow,

Her Snore Ball,
Her miniature Electric Organ,
An' her wonderful Electric Blanket.

Evenin's when the sunlight westers
I pity muh pioneer an-cestors.
They rode the wilderness wide and high,
But how did they ever go sleepy-bye
Without their Eye Shade,
Their Clock-Radio,
Their Sleep Record,
Their Vaporizer,
Their Sinus Mask,
Their Electric Slippers,
Their Yawn Plaque,
Their Slumber Buzzer,
Their Massagin' Pillow,
Their Snore Ball,
Their miniature Electric Organ,
An' their wonderful Electric Blanket?

WHAT THE WELL-READ PATIENT IS TALKING ABOUT

or

LOOK, MA, WHAT I GOT!

The more I leaf through the dictionary in my physician's
waiting room the more my ego grows;
I feel rather like the man who was delighted to find that
all his life he had been speaking prose,
Because I discover that my modest minor ailments,
Why, when expressed in scientific terminology, they are
major physical derailments.
What I thought were merely little old mumps and measles
turn out to have been parotitis and rubella,

And chicken pox, that's for the birds, have I told you about my impressive varicella?
I apologize for my past solecisms, which were heinous,
Never again shall I mention flat feet or bunions when referring to the hallux valgus on my pes planus.
It projects me into a state of hypnosis
To reflect that a watched pot never boils, it furunculosis.
Once my internal rumblings at parties caused me to wish I could shrink to nothing, or at least to a pigmy,
But now I proudly inquire, Can everybody hear my borborygmi?
My one ambition is to become as rich as Croesus,
So that instead of this bourgeois backache I can afford some spondylolisthesis,
Although then I suppose I would look back on my impecunious days with acute nostalgia
Because my headaches would also have progressed from rags to riches, or from Horatio Alger to cephalalgia.
I have certainly increased my learning by more than a smidgin,
Now I know that that specifically projecting Hollywood starlet is not a squab, she's a steatopigeon.
Indeed, I know so much that it would be truly tragic were I to be afflicted with aphasia,
And if you can't swallow that statement it is my diagnosis that you are suffering from achalasia.

WHO'LL BUY MY LINGUAL?
or
YOU PRONOUNCE PLUIE, LOUIE

I wander through a Paris shower,
Off to inspect a flat *à louer.*

The water pours as from a pitcher
On walls inscribed *Défense d'afficher.*

If I have splashed through such a pond,
I don't remember *ou* or *quand.*

With raindrops glistening on my garment,
I reach my goal, I don't know *comment.*

I ring, I do not wish to trespass,
For trespassing is naughty, *n'est-ce pas?*

The stairway irks my fallen arch,
Because one learns *l'ascenseur ne marche.*

I like the flat; with cheerful mien
I murmur to the man, "*Combien?*"

He mentions his idea of payment,
I say that it's exorbitant, *vraiment* —

Have I misunderstood his statement?
I do not speak the French *parfaitement.*

He mentions a reduced emolument,
I cry that it's a deal, *absolument.*

And now I think a glass of wine
Would not be too unpleasant, *hein?*

WHO WANTS TO TRAVEL ALL OVER EUROPE AND SEE NOTHING BUT A LOT OF AMERICAN TOURISTS? I DO

This is the season when I long for a pen as sadly eloquent as Verlaine's,
The season of teeming sea lanes and air lanes,
When life is a round of farewell parties for friends departing toward Venice and Paris
And the Greek islands and the Edinburgh Festival and the Vale of Kashmir, with side trips on the *Kungsholm* and the *Stella Polaris.*
Everybody else is boarding a plane or a liner or a sailing vessel with a real kitchen and baths, and cabins with eight-foot headroom,
And you are pricing air-conditioners for your bedroom,
Which you never get to get, because the economic reasons advanced for staying at home turn out to be a fraud,
Because the going-away presents cost you more than the air-conditioner, and, indeed, as much as a trip abroad.
Here is one Odysseus who is tired of fretting over the cost of a bus trip to Ashtabula,
Who is tired of being an island of indigence in a sea of moola.

Would I were one of that foursome of Texans who wished
to play golf at St. Andrews, far from the land of
their birth,
And the caddie master said he was out of caddies and
they said, Well, just this once we'll go around in
Chevvies, but don't let it get back to Forth Worth.

CROSSING THE BORDER

Senescence begins
And middle age ends
The day your descendants
Outnumber your friends.

INDEX OF FIRST LINES